Existing-Light Photography

Written for Kodak by Hubert C. Birnbaum
and the Editors of Eastman Kodak Company

The KODAK Workshop Series

Helping to expand your understanding of photography

Existing-Light Photography

Written for Kodak by Hubert C. Birnbaum
and the editors of Eastman Kodak Company

Kodak Editor: Caroline A. Grimes

Book Design: Dan J. Malczewski

Front Cover: Art Director, Caroline Grimes
Design, Bill Buckett Associates Inc.
Photographer, Steve Kelly

Consumer/Professional & Finishing Markets
Eastman Kodak Company
Rochester, New York 14650

KODAK Publication KW-17
CAT 144 1179
Library of Congress Catalog Card Number 83-81293
ISBN 0-87985-302-6
5-84-EX New Publication
Printed in the United States of America

*The Kodak materials described in this book are available
from those dealers normally supplying Kodak products. Other materials
may be used, but equivalent results may not be obtained.*

KODAK, KODACOLOR, VR, TRI-X, EKTACHROME, KODACHROME,
FLEXICOLOR, ROYAL-X, PANATOMIC-X, VERICHROME, HOBBY-PAC,
TECHNIDOL, T-GRAIN, PLUS-X, D-76, and INSTAGRAPHIC are trademarks.

Rio de Janeiro, Brazil
Neil Montanus

Contents

Introduction

Neil Montanus

Photographed on KODACOLOR *VR 1000 Film under demanding conditions—action in existing light with a telephoto lens. 1/250 second at f/3.5. Alberto Zoppe'* produced Circus Europa.

Slow photographic plates and films and relatively small-aperture slow-speed lenses made it difficult to take good existing-light pictures in the early days of photography. Neither camera nor subject could move during the long exposures required, as in this example made in the 1860's.

International Museum of Photography
at George Eastman House

In the early days of photography, the ability to make attractive, natural-looking photographs in existing subdued lighting was a tantalizing dream. Lenses of limited light-gathering ability and relatively insensitive plates and films tended to discourage all but the most skilled photographers from attempting to record other than fully lighted outdoor subjects in bright daylight. Many familiar sights and events were, in effect off-limits to most photographers because they took place too early or too late in the day or because they occurred indoors beyond the reach of daylight. Modern high-speed lenses and sensitive high-speed films have for all practical purposes shattered these limitations of time and place, expanding the photographers' world beyond the dreams of their predecessors. Today, with few exceptions, if you can see it, you can photograph it. And it is much easier than you might imagine. In the following pages you'll find practical techniques for taking good pictures in the vast and fascinating world that begins where bright outdoor daylight ends. It is the world of existing-light photography.

Today's sensitive high-speed films and wide-aperture high-speed lenses make it easy to take natural-looking existing-light photographs almost anywhere you can see the subject. And you can often use shutter speeds fast enough to stop even the rapid motion of a circus act. KODACOLOR VR 1000 *Film. Alberto Zoppe' produced* Circus Europa.

John Menihan, Jr.

Existing-Light Photography

EXISTING LIGHT

The term existing-light photography is somewhat difficult to define because it encompasses so much and because its definition is an arbitrary one. First and foremost, it is photography performed primarily with illumination existing in and inherent to the scene. It is usually photography performed under relatively subdued lighting. In terms of these preconditions, the only light sources that don't qualify are bright outdoor daylight and artificial lights that you introduce into the scene as primary sources of illumination. Living room lamps, fluorescent lights in stores and offices, arc lights at a circus or ice show, vapor lamps on city streets, lighted signs, firelight from a campfire, skylight flooding through a window, and candles flickering on a restaurant table are all examples of existing-light sources.

Skylight—Daylight

Arc Lights, Ice Capades, Inc.

Living Room Lamps—Tungsten Light

Fluorescent Lights

Norm Kerr

Elaine Rutkowski, KINSA*

Sunlight

*Courtesy Kodak International Newspaper Snapshot Awards

Vapor Lamps

Neil Montanus

Outdoors at Night—Twilight

Neil Montanus

Brian Speer

Candlelight

Existing light is the light inherent in the scene, whatever it may be. It is less bright than most outdoor daylight conditions and is often quite dim.

7

Technically, existing light covers all natural lighting—from moonlight to bright sunshine. For photography, though, we're going to limit the definition of existing light to mean lighting situations characterized by lower light levels that require considerably more exposure than for subjects in most outdoor daylight lighting conditions. Photography in outdoor daylight is excluded from the existing-light category because basic picture-taking can be done in daylight with all cameras without the special techniques required for low-light situations. If the term existing light included outdoor daylight, it would lose its meaning.

Existing-light photography is sometimes called available-light photography. Because the word available opens a rather large loophole in that any extraneous lighting a photographer chooses to use or take along could be considered available, even if it becomes the primary light source, the term existing-light photography is less ambiguous and will be used throughout this book. Note, too, that some photographers, in deference to the dim-light aspects of many existing-light situations, have also dubbed it unavailable-light photography. Admittedly, it sometimes seems that way.

Existing-Light Pleasures and Perils

One of the best reasons for photographing by existing light is that the resulting pictures can have a natural look that is extremely difficult or impossible to re-create with contrived lighting. Existing-light photographs are unexcelled for preserving the mood of a scene. The final picture will nearly always evoke the feelings you associated with the natural appearance of the setting, in addition to revealing the people and things before the lens in a realistic way.

The cloud that accompanies the silver lining is that illumination we consider perfectly acceptable as part of a particular

Bruce Nett

environment, such as the lighting in homes, in the work place, and in public places indoors, and outdoors at night, may be marginal or worse in purely photographic terms. While the existing illumination is usually sufficient for its intended purpose of lighting the environment, it's often contrasty, uneven, and dim for photography. In following pages you will learn to cope with many of the less favorable characteristics of existing light. For the moment, though, let's accept the premise that even an exceptionally attractive existing-light photograph will not necessarily embody all the classical photographic virtues of high technical quality and perfection that you would expect to find in an artfully contrived studio simulation of a similar scene. The

outstanding attribute of existing-light photography is its natural portrayal of the scene. This usually more than compensates for some necessary compromise in technical quality to achieve this kind of photograph.

Sometimes using existing light is the only practical way to photograph a subject. It's usually not possible to use flash to photograph scenes such as large building interiors or distant lighted subjects outdoors at night. The light from the flash just won't reach that far.

TWO BASIC WAYS TO USE EXISTING LIGHT

There are two fundamentally different approaches you can take to existing-light photography. Most photographers use both, choosing one or the other according to circumstances and photographic intent.

The first might be characterized as a journalistic approach, in which large-aperture high-speed lenses and high-speed films are employed to permit shooting freely with a handheld camera. This method allows you great freedom of movement and encourages spontaneous shooting that can result in photographs of great charm and vitality. You can aim your camera freely and not be encumbered by using a camera support. To many photographers, existing-light photography is synonymous with the journalistic approach.

The second way of photographing by existing light could be thought of as a traditional approach, since it is reminiscent of the working methods all photographers used in the early days before high-speed lenses and films were available. With this technique you put your camera on a tripod or other firm camera support for maximum steadiness during relatively long exposures with slow shutter speeds or time exposures. This lets you use almost any lens, since you may be using a moderate to small aperture to enhance depth of field, and a medium- or low-speed film for optimum sharpness and freedom from graininess. See the picture on the next page. These films usually have better sharpness and graininess characteristics than higher-speed film. In exchange for giving up journalistic freedom of movement, you may be able to make sharper, finer-grained pictures with

Flash pictures, while adequate to record many scenes, have an artificial appearance due to the flat, frontal lighting (top). Existing-light pictures taken in the natural lighting are much better at portraying scenes as they appear.

Bob Clemens

The natural look is the hallmark of existing-light photographs. Here, an existing-light picture of a play (left) is technically less elegant, but more realistic looking, than a professionally lighted and arranged studio photograph of a dancer made by a professional photographer. Both photos are excellent examples but represent two different approaches to photography.

Caroline Grimes

Gary Whelpley

Keith Boas

Caroline Grimes

2.8

improved depth of field. These photographs can withstand considerable enlargement or projection on a screen to very large size.

The journalistic approach is the method of choice for capturing fluid situations in which motion must be followed or stopped as in candid or action photography. This is the method to use when you want to take many pictures from many different points of view in a short period, and you don't have the time or space to use a camera support. The traditional method is the one to use for relatively static scenes when maximum image quality takes precedence over concern with photographing candid situations or stopping motion. The traditional technique may be the method to choose for situations when you have more time to set up your camera on a camera support and make careful observations and adjustments for best framing and composition. These clear-cut distinctions notwithstanding, you will find examples later in this book in which elements of both shooting styles are combined to meet specific picture requirements. Existing-light photography is very much an art of compromise.

High-speed films and large aperture lenses let you photograph freely with a handheld camera to capture the vibrancy of life around you, much as a photojournalist would. The journalistic approach lets you take pictures rapidly, conveniently, unobtrusively, and in locations where camera supports or flash may be impractical to use or may not be permitted.

A medium-speed, fine-grained film, KODACHROME 64 Film (Daylight), recorded this scene very sharply, preserving fine detail, during a relatively long exposure made with a slow shutter speed. The camera was mounted on a tripod.

CAMERAS FOR EXISTING-LIGHT PHOTOGRAPHY

Strictly speaking, almost any camera in proper operating condition is capable of making acceptable pictures under at least some existing-light circumstances. However, if you want to deal with the broad spectrum of existing-light situations efficiently and conveniently, the following attributes and capabilities are desirable, although a camera needn't embody all of them to perform satisfactorily.

Single-lens reflex cameras are excellent cameras for existing-light photography because they have through-the-lens viewing and focusing, precise viewfinder framing, and the capability for using different, interchangeable lenses.

Rangefinder cameras are also a good choice for existing-light photos, although the reasons may not be quite as obvious. These non-SLR cameras, which have direct optical viewfinders, feature faster, more accurate focusing, quieter operation, smaller size, and lighter weight. They are less obtrusive for candid shots and are easier to carry. An additional advantage is that, unlike SLR cameras, the viewfinder on a rangefinder camera does not go blank when the exposure is made. The photographer's view of the subject remains uninterrupted at the most critical time—the moment you take the picture.

Non-SLR cameras with automatic focusing or manual distance-scale focusing also offer many of the same advantages as rangefinder cameras.

A camera that lets you compose and focus quickly and easily in dim light is an advantage in existing-light photography. And the clearer the display of camera functions, the better. With an SLR camera, a high-speed lens with a large maximum lens opening helps make the viewfinder image brighter.

Bright Viewing

Since much existing-light photography is done in relatively dim conditions, a viewfinder that presents you with an easy-to-see viewing/focusing image will facilitate composing and focusing accurately. Any vital information about camera functions displayed in the finder should be easy to see, too. If you're using a single-lens reflex camera, a high-speed lens with a maximum lens opening of $f/2$ or larger is beneficial for making the image on the viewfinder screen brighter.

Accurate Focusing

The focusing device should be sufficiently large and bright to permit easy use in dark areas. Although you can use fixed-focus cameras and models that require estimating subject distance, subjects at close and medium distances in dim light require accurate focus setting to be recorded sharply. Automatic focusing systems built into some cameras or into some interchangeable lenses for single-lens reflex (SLR) cameras may not function reliably in very low light levels. If you have an auto-focus camera or lens, check the owner's manual to see if the system is suited to use in fairly dark surroundings. If not, focus manually if you can with your equipment.

Here again a high-speed lens is a big plus for an SLR camera. Since you focus with the lens wide open at its maximum lens opening, depth of field is very shallow which makes it easier to judge when you have the lens adjusted for sharp focus.

Sensitive Exposure Meter

A sensitive built-in exposure meter, or light meter, or a separate handheld meter that reads accurately in dim light will increase your yield of well exposed pictures. A hand-held exposure meter is especially helpful if your in-camera meter is not sensitive enough to give a reliable reading in dim lighting or if your camera does not have a built-in light meter. For scenes too dim, too complex, or too inaccessible to permit making useful exposure readings with a meter, tables of suggested existing-light exposures in following chapters will see you through.

Adjustable shutter speeds you can set directly by turning a shutter speed dial or indirectly through other camera controls enhance your ability to handhold your camera and still obtain proper exposure, and to photograph motion, depending on the situation. For dim-light shooting, it's helpful if the shutter provides a range of timed speeds down to 1 second or longer plus a B setting for time exposures with a camera support.

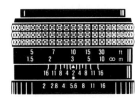

Adjusting the lens aperture increases or decreases the amount of light the lens transmits to the film during any given period of time. Apertures of f/2.8 and larger are desirable for existing-light photography in dim surroundings in order to let you use shutter speeds fast enough for handholding your camera.

Adjustable Shutter and Lens

Adjustable shutter speeds and f/stops, whether set by you or by the camera, increase your ability to deal with existing-light situations. If you have a camera with automatic exposure control, it's handy to be able to override the automation or make settings manually in lighting that might fool the camera exposure system. If you anticipate photographing

often in very low light, a shutter that provides timed speeds down to 1 second as well as a B setting for longer exposures increases your photographic options.

Tripod Socket

A tripod socket in the camera body permits mounting the camera on a tripod or other camera support with a screw-type fitting when taking pictures at shutter speeds too slow for handheld photography. If your camera doesn't have a tripod socket, you can improvise ways to brace it during long exposures (see "Camera-Handling Techniques," page 20.)

LENSES

In terms of suitability for convenient existing-light use, the most important attribute of a lens is its light-gathering ability. A lens with a reasonably large maximum aperture, such as f/2.8 or larger, will let you work at faster shutter speeds in dim light than one with a smaller maximum aperture. With high-speed film in your camera, you will be able to take more pictures with the camera handheld, and in all cases the higher shutter speeds allowed will contribute to greater picture sharpness by counteracting subject and/or camera movement. Most modern 35 mm and other handheld cameras are equipped with or may be fitted with normal focal-length lenses of f/2.8 or larger maximum aperture. Much faster normal focal-length lenses, with apertures ranging between f/2 and f/1.2, are generally available for interchangeable-lens 35 mm cameras.

If you have an interchangeable-lens camera and several lenses, select the fastest optics for existing-light use, particularly if the camera is a single-lens reflex. Shutter-speed considerations aside, the brighter view through a larger aperture will make focusing and composing much easier in dim surroundings.

Wide-Angle Lenses

Wide-angle lenses, which include more of a scene at a given distance than a normal focal-length lens, are helpful when shooting in confined areas indoors or when you want to capture a broad view of the outdoor world. A distinct bonus of wide-angle lenses is that they minimize the effects of minor camera movement, allowing sharp pictures to be made with a

Norm Kerr

A wide-angle lens lets you record more of the scene on film without moving farther away from the subject, so is very useful in confined interiors. Here a wide-angle lens expanded a setting optically to show the statue relative to its surroundings.

handheld camera at lower-than-usual shutter speeds. A wide-angle lens offers another advantage of increased depth of field for the same camera-to-subject distance when compared with a lens of longer focal length used at the same lens opening.

A wide-angle lens is good to use when you want to shoot fast and you don't have time to adjust the focus with the camera rangefinder. Since a wide-angle lens is less critical for focus than longer focal-length lenses, you can just estimate the subject distance quickly and set the lens focusing scale. These lenses are so forgiving that with practice, you may be able to shoot candid shots without looking through the viewfinder to help obtain unposed expressions.

Norm Kerr

A telephoto lens lets you make a larger image on film without moving closer, bridging the distance optically. Hold cameras with telephoto lenses steady because they magnify camera motion along with the image. Also, pay particular attention to focusing accurately because depth of field is shallow with these lenses.

Telephoto Lenses

Telephoto lenses help you approach and isolate your subject without actually moving closer by projecting a larger image on the film. In so doing, they also magnify camera movement and require extra-steady holding and the use of higher-than-normal shutter speeds for best sharpness.

Generally, because existing light is characterized by low light levels, the use of telephoto lenses with a handheld camera is limited to some extent. Exposures for most existing-light pictures require large lens openings and relatively slow shutter speeds. Many telephoto lenses and zoom lenses have smaller maximum apertures than normal focal-length lenses, and require higher shutter speeds for handheld photography. For these reasons the use of a telephoto lens is limited to focal lengths of about 150 mm or less with a handheld camera. A camera support is necessary for telephoto lenses of longer focal length or whenever the light is too dim to permit a high enough shutter speed to use the camera handheld. See page 22.

When you use a telephoto lens, depth of field will be shallower than if you used a lens of shorter focal length at the same camera-to-subject distance and f/stop. If good depth of field is required for your subject, don't use a telephoto lens handheld. Focusing is more critical with a telephoto lens because of the shallow depth of field, so focus carefully.

Here, a 35-105 mm focal-length zoom lens on a 35 mm camera was used at 35 mm wide-angle (top), 50 mm normal (center), and 105 mm telephoto (bottom) settings from a fixed distance. To obtain sharp pictures and avoid the blurred effects of camera motion while using a zoom lens at the telephoto settings on a handheld camera, you should use high shutter speeds. At the 35 mm wide-angle position you could use 1/30 second, but at the 105 mm telephoto position you would need to use 1/125 second for handholding your camera.

Tom Beelma

Zoom Lenses

Zoom lenses are very convenient because they let you change image size on the film continuously over a range that may run from wide-angle to telephoto without changing your distance from the subject and without physically changing lenses. Many zoom lenses have maximum apertures smaller than $f/2.8$ and are therefore not well suited to handheld photography in low light. You may be able to use zoom lenses effectively, though, when conditions permit employing a tripod or other firm camera support. Some zoom lenses have, in effect, more than one maximum aperture. At the short end of the focal-length range the maximum aperture may be $f/2.8$, for example, but then reduce gradually to $f/3.5$ or smaller as you shift the focal length toward the long end of the range.

If you're using a zoom lens with a handheld camera in dim light and trying to manage by using the slowest feasible shutter speed, then try to stay with the shorter focal-length settings. If you're using the telephoto setting, be sure that your shutter speed is high enough to obtain a sharp picture. See page 22. It's a common pitfall to overlook this condition with an aperture-preferred automatic camera, which determines the shutter speed depending on the lens opening you select. It's very easy to forget to check whether the shutter speed the camera is selecting is high enough for handholding your camera with a zoom lens set on telephoto. The slower shutter speeds may be quite adequate for the shorter focal-length settings of the zoom lens, but not for the longer focal length settings.

USEFUL ACCESSORIES

Most of the time, a suitable camera, lens, and film are all you need to make satisfactory existing-light pictures. Every now and then, though, having the right accessory can make the difference between getting the picture you want and having to settle for something less. The following accessories are basic aids to good existing-light photography.

Tripods

When the light is too low to make sharp pictures without camera motion with a handheld camera, use a tripod if conditions permit. Mounting your camera on a tripod when you have to use slow shutter speeds or time exposures helps you make the sharpest possible pictures. Tripods come in all sizes from pocketable mini models to comparatively huge heavyweights. A small tabletop tripod can be a permanent resident in your equipment bag as a form of low-light insurance. These small, compact tripods are fast and easy to use. You can press the base against a wall, a tabletop, or similar surface, or even your chest to help steady your camera. The mini tripods are usually faster to use and easier to carry but may not be as steady as the larger, heavier tripods. Full-size models provide maximum versatility and stability when their size and weight are not inhibiting factors for you.

When you can foresee the need for a tripod, take a full-size model with you for increased steadiness. Since the main reason for using a tripod of any size is to support the camera steadily, look for a tripod that has rigidity and stability as well as portability.

Camera Clamps

A camera clamp screw-mounts to the camera's tripod socket and lets you position the camera firmly by locking the jaws on any strong, immobile object that's the right size and in the right place. Depending on the clamp jaws, you may be able to mount the camera on a car door or window, on a fence rail or on the back of a chair. Take care that the jaws don't mar objects of value.

A camera clamp can provide firm support in places where tripods are prohibited or cannot be used for reasons of convenience or safety. KODACOLOR VR 400 *Film.*

Bean Bags and Shot Bags

Small bean bags and canvas bags filled with fine lead birdshot can be good improvised camera props when more rigid supports are unavailable or cannot be used. Work the camera gently against the bag until it nestles in a form-fitting depression, then squeeze the bag to adjust the camera position when refining composition. If you don't have a bean bag with you, you can use a folded jacket, a soft hat that you can crumple, a soft camera bag, or a book to rest your camera on for picture-taking.

Bruce Nett

A bean bag or small bag filled with fine lead shot makes a formfitting prop for your camera during long exposures. Squeeze or poke the bag gently to make small changes in camera position. Or you can improvise and use a crumpled-up jacket or soft hat for the same purpose. Here a bean bag is supported by a post. KODACOLOR VR 200 *Film.*

Cable Release

A cable release lets you trip the shutter of a camera mounted on a tripod or other type of support without risking camera movement from the touch of your finger. A supple cable release about 12 inches (30.5 cm) long or longer can sag limply or form a rainbow curve between hand and camera, damping your motion effectively.

A locking type cable release is beneficial for making time exposures when you're using the "B" shutter setting on your camera. This will keep the shutter open on B until you release the lock. Some cameras have a "T," or TIME, setting which opens the shutter when you push the release button and holds it open until you push the release a second time. Keep a cable release in your equipment bag and another with your tripod, perhaps taped to one of the legs. That way you'll be sure to have one when needed. Instead of using a cable release, you can let the camera self timer make the exposure.

Small Flash Unit

Although the essence of existing-light photography is making pictures by the natural lighting on the scene, it's sometimes desirable to lighten shadows that would otherwise record too dark in contrasty lighting. Strictly speaking, this is not true existing-light photography, but the pictures appear very similar to those that are. A small, relatively low-power electronic flash unit or a unit that has a light output reduction switch will let you lighten the shadows easily. If you have a camera, such as a KODAK Disc Camera, with a built-in flash unit, you won't need another flash unit for that camera. The technique for using flash fill is described in the chapter "Existing-Light Pictures at Home."

Pocket Flashlight

Tuck a pocket flashlight in your pocket, purse, or camera bag when setting forth in search of existing-light subjects. It will help you see what you're doing when the ambient light is too dim for reading shutter speeds, f/stops, and exposure guides. It will also help you find anything you drop in the dark.

Spare Batteries

Modern photographic equipment lives on batteries. Keep a spare set of batteries for all your battery-powered photo equipment. Take spares with you, even if your picture outing is just for a few hours and within walking distance of home so you won't be caught short by unanticipated battery failure. If you're using rechargeable batteries make sure they are adequately charged. It seems that batteries never fail when replacements are readily available.

Lens Cleaning Materials

Clean lenses make sharper images than dirty ones, particularly in existing-light conditions. Check your lenses regularly to make sure exposed glass surfaces are free of dust and fingerprints. A soft, clean lens brush removes dust safely. Stubborn specks and fingerprints can be removed with KODAK Lens Cleaner and Lens Cleaning Paper. Don't use chemically treated eyeglass cleaning tissues because they are not designed for cleaning camera lenses and may remove the anti-reflection coating on the outer surface of the lens.

Lens Shades

Although lens shades are not a necessity for most existing-light pictures, they are useful in two different ways. They shield the lens from strong light outside the picture field, reducing internal lens reflections, and promoting sharper, more sparkling pictures. And they provide some physical protection for the front surface of the lens against dust, dirt, and contact with foreign objects. If you have several lenses and lens shades, be sure to use the right shade for each lens. A shallow lens shade intended for a wide-angle lens provides insufficient shielding for a normal or telephoto lens. A deeper, narrower shade made for a telephoto will vignette, or cut off, the corners and sometimes the edges of the picture if you use it on a wide-angle lens.

Properly designed lens shades can keep stray light from degrading image quality and also offer some physical protection to the lens surface. Match the right shade with the right lens if you own several.

Pocket Notebook and Pencil

The best way to ensure repeating successful working methods and to avoid repeating mistakes when refining a new technique or photographing in difficult or unfamiliar conditions is to take notes as you take pictures. Keep a small notebook and pen or pencil with your photo gear for recording pertinent data, such as subject, type of film you used, exposure settings the meter recommended, and what you actually did. And by all means write down when and where you take pictures while traveling. That way you'll know whether the dancers in the café were celebrating in Paris or Madrid, Rome, Italy or Rome, New York.

An extremely broad selection of films for general photography is available from Eastman Kodak Company. Nearly all are applicable to existing-light photography, according to the kind of pictures you want—prints or slides, color or black-and-white—and to your taste and requirements imposed by specific picture-taking circumstances.

FILMS FOR EXISTING-LIGHT PHOTOGRAPHY

Eastman Kodak Company supplies an extraordinary variety of films for general photography. Nearly all are applicable to existing-light photography, according to the kinds of photos you want and to your taste, and the requirements imposed by specific picture-taking circumstances.

Generally, the films are differentiated according to the kind of pictures they make—color or black-and-white—traditional or instant—and prints or slides. The kinds of film can also be categorized broadly according to their sensitivity to light—film speed—and to their color balance.

Sensitivity to Light

A film that is highly sensitive to light, commonly called a high-speed, or fast, film, requires comparatively little exposure to light to form a useful image. Films that are relatively less sensitive to light, generally referred to as medium-speed and low-speed films, require correspondingly greater exposure to light to form useful images.

In bright, conventional light—outdoors in the daytime—low- and medium-speed general-purpose films are fast enough to allow photographing active subjects with a handheld camera. In progressively dimmer light, such as existing light, high-speed films continue to provide the convenience of handholding the camera while capturing motion sharply on film. The fast films offer increased depth of field with smaller lens openings as well as the opportunity to shoot existing-light action shots at higher shutter speeds.

Since most people prefer the freedom of photographing with a handheld camera in a variety of lighting conditions, high-speed films are the mainstay for existing-light photography. However, medium- and low-speed films can still be used, provided the existing light is relatively bright and you don't have to stop motion with fast shutter speeds, or provided you steady the camera with a tripod or an improvised support and use slow shutter speeds or time exposures when the existing light is dim.

Tom Beelmann

For the picture above, KODACHROME 25 Film (Daylight), ISO (ASA) 25, was fast enough to make an informal portrait in bright existing light with a handheld camera. During a circus act, however, the photographer needed the extra speed of KODAK EKTACHROME 400 Film (Daylight), with ESP-1 Processing, ISO (ASA) 800, to make a handheld action-stopping shot. M & M Circus International.

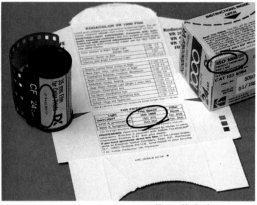

Harvey Harland

Film speeds are provided for Kodak films on the film carton, on the film instructions, and on some film containers.

Film Speeds

Film sensitivity is determined by the manufacturer according to standard procedures. In the United States and some other parts of the world, film sensitivity is expressed in terms of ISO (ASA) speed numbers. The higher the film-speed number, the greater the sensitivity of the film. For example, a film rated at a speed of ISO (ASA) 1000 is two and a half times as sensitive as one rated at ISO (ASA) 400, and ten times as sensitive as a film rated at ISO (ASA) 100. Be sure to set the film-speed dial on your camera or your handheld exposure meter to the correct speed number for the film you are using.

Some film manufacturers outside the United States express film sensitivity in ISO° (DIN) numbers. Kodak provides ISO, ASA, and DIN numbers on some film cartons. Only ISO speed numbers are given on film cartons and instructions for color-negative film for color prints. Eventually ASA and DIN speeds will be discontinued. The relationship between ISO (ASA) film speeds, which is an arithmetic system, and ISO° (DIN) film speeds, which is a logarithmic system, is shown in the table on the next page. Since the primary film-speed system in the U.S.A. is ISO (ASA), most of the equipment sold in the U.S.A. is designed for use with this system. However, some of this equipment has both speed systems included. If your in-camera meter or separate exposure meter has film speed scales for both speed systems, be sure to set the applicable film speed number on the appropriate scale or gross exposure error can result.

Martin Czamanske

Caroline Grimes

ISO (ASA)/ISO (DIN) FILM SPEEDS

ISO (ASA)	ISO (DIN)	ISO (ASA)	ISO (DIN)
6	9°	160	23°
8	10°	200	24°
10	11°	250	25°
12	12°	320	26°
16	13°	400	27°
20	14°	500	28°
25	15°	640	29°
32	16°	800	30°
40	17°	1000	31°
50	18°	1250	32°
64	19°	1600	33°
80	20°	2000	34°
100	21°	2500	35°
125	22°	3200	36°

Arithmetic ISO (ASA) film speed numbers can differ greatly from the equivalent logarithmic ISO° (DIN) film speed numbers. Note that ISO° (DIN) numbers used in some countries outside the United States are followed by a degree symbol (°). For example, when film speed is given as ISO 400/27°, 400 is the former ASA value and 27 is the former DIN value.

Kodak films rated at ISO (ASA) 800 to 1600 are designated very high-speed and those at ISO (ASA) 250 to 640 are considered high-speed films. Those rated at ISO (ASA) 200 down to ISO (ASA) 64 are considered to be medium speed, and films with still lower speed numbers, ISO (ASA) 50 and below, are generally referred to as low-speed films.

Kodak films with ISO (ASA) speeds of 160 and higher are good choices for existing-light photography because they allow brief exposures even in fairly dim lighting. The very high-speed films, such as KODACOLOR VR 1000 Film, ISO 1000, and high-speed films, such as KODAK EKTACHROME 400 Film (Daylight), ISO (ASA) 400, will let you photograph easily almost anything you can see while handholding your camera, depending on its exposure capabilities. Medium-speed films at the upper end of the category, such as KODACOLOR VR 100, ISO 100, and others with ISO (ASA) speeds from approximately 100 up to 200, allow handheld photography in relatively

In bright existing light, you can use a medium-speed film for handheld photography if you don't need a great deal of action-stopping capability or depth of field. Here the photographer exposed KODAK EKTACHROME 100 Film (Daylight) for 1/60 second at f/2.8.

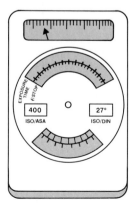

If your exposure meter has film-speed scales for both ISO (ASA) and ISO° (DIN) speed numbers, be sure to set the right number on the right scale. Otherwise, considerable exposure error can result.

John Menihan, Jr.

Use a very high-speed film to stop action in low light. Here the photographer exposed KODACOLOR VR 1000 Film, ISO 1000, in a handheld camera at 1/500 second and f/2.8.

John Phelps

To make this picture, the photographer exposed KODACHROME 64 Film (Daylight), ISO (ASA) 64, in a tripod-mounted camera using a time exposure. The long exposure let the moving amusement park ride create a colorful blur, while the sharp, fine-grain film recorded the stationary elements in the scene in detail. An exposure of 2 seconds produced this effect.

bright existing light, but may require you to use a tripod for best results in dim conditions. Medium-speed films at the lower end of the category and low-speed films, such as KODACHROME 64 Film (Daylight), ISO (ASA) 64, and KODACHROME 25 Film (Daylight), ISO (ASA) 25, provide superb picture quality when you can use a tripod and the subject permits using slow shutter speeds or time exposures. You may also be able to use medium- and low-speed films for handheld photography in bright light conditions, such as window light.

As a general rule for existing-light photography with a handheld camera, use the fastest film you can, all other factors being equal. There are many valid exceptions to this rule. Examples of the rule and exceptions to it occur frequently throughout this book.

Boosting Film-Speed Numbers

Although the ISO (ASA) speed of a film accurately represents its sensitivity as determined by standard test procedures, some films may be made to behave as

though they were substantially more sensitive than the ISO (ASA) speed indicates. The procedure, called push processing, consists of underexposing the film by a specific amount and then extending development to help compensate for the underexposure. KODAK EKTACHROME Films for color slides and KODAK TRI-X Pan Film for black-and-white prints respond very well, with qualifications, to moderate pushing under certain conditions. The technique will be covered in greater detail in the chapter "KODAK Films for Existing-Light Photography." Unlike reversal, or color-slide films, color-negative films, such as KODACOLOR films, do not accomodate push-processing techniques and are not recommended for that use. As a rule, it is preferable to use a high-speed film at its normal speed rather than to push-process a slower speed film to a higher speed number to match it.

Color Rendition

The first distinction to make among films with regard to color rendition is whether they produce pictures in color or in black-and-white.

Black-and-White Films

Since black-and-white films, such as KODAK TRI-X Pan Film, translate the colors in the scene into appropriately light or dark shades of gray and have good exposure latitude as well, the films are simple to use for existing-light photography. For all practical purposes, it doesn't really matter whether the subject is illuminated by standard daylight, bluish skylight, yellow-orange incandescent tungsten lamps, or fluorescent tubes of different color qualities. Colors you remember as light will be rendered as light tones of gray; colors that appeared dark will be rendered as darker tones of gray; and extremely light or dark parts of the scene will be rendered as white and black, respectively.

The ability of black-and-white films to produce plausible-looking, although monochromatic pictures, in virtually any commonly encountered lighting makes them very well suited to existing-light photography. No matter what sort of lights or odd combinations of lights illuminate a scene, you can usually photograph freely in black and white without

17

Margaret Summers, KINSA

Color Films

The other principal class of films consists of those that produce finished pictures in color. Two further major subdivisions are films that produce color negatives intended primarily for making color prints, and films that are processed into positive color slides, or transparencies. Color films capture the color of the light illuminating the scene. The sometimes subtle differences in the color of the illumination, while usually of no significance with black-and-white film, are important for pictures taken on color film. Color films exaggerate the color differences between light sources used for general illumination in color photographs. This happens because our eyes are more forgiving when we view the scenes directly and we tend to minimize the variations in the color quality of the illumination from one scene to another.

Generally, a good film to use for handheld existing-light photography is one with a high film speed combined with good graininess and sharpness qualities. KODAK TRI-X Pan Film is an excellent choice for this purpose when you want black-and-white prints.

having to take special precautions to secure a realistic gray-tone rendition. Also, great opportunity for contrast control exists in the black-and-white printing process, which allows making satisfactory prints from negatives that have recorded high-contrast or low-contrast subject matter.

Black-and-white films have great potential to produce dramatic, artistic renditions with a rich range of black-and-white tones. Even though black-and-white photographs cannot be true representations of the scenes' appearance in color, we readily accept black-and-white photos because we are so accustomed to seeing them. Pictures from the early days of photography are mostly black-and-white and many photographers still choose black-and-white as the medium for expressing their creative talents in the art of photography.

Bruce

There are important differences between the way color films perform, especially for existing-light photography. Color negative film has more exposure latitude and more tolerance for color differences of light sources because corrections can be made during the printing process. Color slide film is more critical for both exposure and for matching the color of the light source *to the color balance of the film, because the processed film you get back as a color slide is the film that you exposed in your camera. Here KODACOLOR VR 1000 Film has handled the combination of tungsten lighting and the faint glow of daylight in the sky at dusk very well.*

Color-Negative Films Are Versatile

To a remarkable extent, color-negative films, such as KODACOLOR VR 1000 Film, are universal films in that they are capable of providing good color reproduction under most common existing-light situations and rendering scene colors well under the more difficult lighting conditions when color rendition in your photographs is not critical. This owes in large part to the considerable scope that exists in color printing to correct and otherwise manipulate color rendition in the final print. The printing stage also permits some contrast control through choice of printing paper. These qualities make color-negative films very useful in existing-light photography. Whether your intent is to reproduce the scene as closely as possible or to interpret it as fancifully as you can, a single negative and careful printing can carry you from the real to the surreal.

Color-Slide Films Should Match the Light Source

To obtain realistic color rendition with color-slide materials, such as KODAK EKTACHROME and KODACHROME Films, you should match the color balance of the film with the appropriate light source, or if there's a mismatch, use a color filter to adjust the quality of the light entering the camera when there's sufficient light and correct color rendition is important. Color-slide films are balanced for use with daylight or with various types of tungsten, or incandescent, illumination. Daylight color-slide films produce strongly yellow-orange results when exposed under tungsten lighting without the proper correction filter. Tungsten color-slide films, which are balanced to produce realistic color rendition with tungsten illumination, produce excessively blue pictures when exposed in daylight or with electronic flash, which is similar to daylight in color quality. Since the film you expose in the camera becomes the finished color slide after processing, there is no intermediate stage during which extensive color corrections or deliberate deviations may be made.

Although it's generally desirable to match film and light source in the interests of realism, ambient illumination in existing-light locales rarely conforms precisely to the standard light sources for which color-slide films are balanced. And frequently several different and theoretically incompatible light sources illuminate the same area simultaneously. That shouldn't be cause for despair or discourage you from using color-slide films when your needs will be served better by slides rather than by prints. The object of most, and indeed the most interesting, existing-light photographs is to evoke the natural appearance of the scene, not necessarily to reproduce it literally, tone for tone and color for color.

FILTERS

For most of existing-light photography it's generally impractical to use filters because of the diversity of light sources and the loss of light through the filter. This makes it difficult to obtain sufficient exposure when using a handheld camera. In addition, there are often light sources of different color quality present in the same scene which further complicates the use of filters. The realism of the existing lighting compensates to a large extent for color rendition that may be less than ideal.

Filter information is included in this book, however, for use when critical color rendition is important for your picture requirements, and you are willing to accept the loss of light through the filter and the restrictions this imposes on your picture-taking techniques.

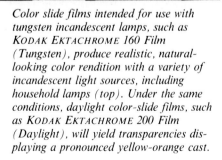

Color slide films intended for use with tungsten incandescent lamps, such as KODAK EKTACHROME 160 Film (Tungsten), produce realistic, natural-looking color rendition with a variety of incandescent light sources, including household lamps (top). Under the same conditions, daylight color-slide films, such as KODAK EKTACHROME 200 Film (Daylight), will yield transparencies displaying a pronounced yellow-orange cast.

When daylight is the dominant light source, a daylight color-slide film, in this case KODAK EKTACHROME 200 Film (Daylight), produces natural-looking color rendition (top). Exposing an artificial-light color slide film, such as KODAK EKTACHROME 160 Film (Tungsten), to daylight results in a picture with a cold, bluish cast.

Camera-Handling Techniques

HOW TO MAKE SHARPER PICTURES IN LOW LIGHT

Since most existing-light photography takes place in lower light levels than are usually encountered in everyday outdoor shooting in the daytime, shutter speeds are generally slower than the speeds you are accustomed to using. And often you will use wider lens apertures than usual to make the most of minimal lighting. As a result, existing-light photography places greater demands on your ability to hold the camera steady, focus accurately, and generally employ the tools and techniques of photography. In fact, though, you don't have to learn anything new and exotic. The following hints for making sharper pictures in low light simply require paying slightly greater attention to the things you ought to be doing already in general picture-taking.

Caroline Grimes

CAMERA STEADINESS

Take a Steady Stance

Holding a camera steadily begins at ground level. Stand with your feet about 18 inches (0.5 m) apart and your weight evenly distributed for a steady stance. Stand comfortably erect and bring the camera viewfinder to your eye. Don't duck or slouch to meet it part way. To the extent that the camera design permits, keep your elbows tucked in close to your body for additional steadiness. Pressing the camera lightly against your face helps, too, but don't overdo it. If you press too hard, you may induce tremors from tension and fatigue.

With normal focal-length or wide-angle lenses many people find that their grip is steadier when they hold the camera body on both sides with their fingers on the front and thumbs on the back. If your camera is equipped with a telephoto or zoom lens that is significantly longer and/or heavier than a normal lens, use your left hand to support the lens rather than holding the camera body. This conveniently positions your left hand for adjusting the focus and/or zoom control on the lens.

Some photographers prefer to use a similar method for short, light lenses, too. Rest the base of the camera body on the heel of your hand and grasp the lens focusing collar with your fingers. Try both camera-holding methods with short, light lenses—the one just described and grasping the camera body on both sides—and choose the one that you find most steady and convenient to use. To determine how steady you're holding your camera, perform the camera-holding test described on page 22.

Learning how to hold your camera steady lets you take sharp pictures with a handheld camera at the relatively slow shutter speeds necessary for proper exposure in existing light. Photographed through a multi-image lens attachment at 1/30 second f/4 on KODAK EKTACHROME 160 Film (Tungsten).

Brace Yourself

The delightful suppleness of the human body makes it a mediocre camera support when slow shutter speeds must be used. You can gain appreciable steadiness by taking advantage of your surroundings. Lean against a pillar or wall, rest the base of the camera on the back of a chair, a railing, or the hood of a car, or prop your elbows on a table. You may feel conspicuous doing so at first, but the sharper pictures you make will help dispel any lingering reluctance you may have.

When using a short, light lens, you can support your camera steadily by grasping the camera body on both sides with your hands. With long, heavier lenses, position your left hand forward under the lens to support its weight.

You'll be able to hold your camera more steadily if you keep your elbows tucked in close to your body with your feet somewhat apart.

Bruce Nett

For extra steadiness at slow shutter speeds, brace yourself against or rest the camera on any firm support you can find.

Release the Shutter Gently

Use a light touch on the shutter release to avoid jarring the camera at the moment of exposure. For the smoothest release, increase pressure on the button gently and steadily until the shutter trips. Another way to release the shutter with even less chance of moving the camera is to use the self-timer and let the camera actuate the shutter. This lets you concentrate on holding the camera steady while the self-timer makes the exposure for you.

Set the self-timer for a shorter than normal interval so you don't have to wait for an excessively long time for the shutter to trip. This self-timer technique is most beneficial when photographing stationary objects, or when using shutter speeds that are borderline for being fast enough to handhold your camera.

Hold Your Breath

Proper breath control is as important to the existing-light photographer as it is to the Olympic sharpshooter. Just before releasing the shutter, take a deep breath, exhale until you feel comfortable, then hold your breath until you've tripped the shutter. You don't want your lungs expanding or contracting to cause body and camera motion at the time the exposure is made.

Check Your Steadiness

You can monitor your progress when you practice handholding your camera without actually exposing any film. Tape a small mirror to your camera at about a 45° angle to the lens axis, as shown in the accompanying illustration. Set up a flashlight or slide projector in a slightly darkened room to shine from one side toward the mirror while you're holding the camera in shooting position. The mirror will reflect the light beam toward the wall at which you aim the lens. Observe the patch of light while releasing the shutter. The less movement you see, the more steadily you are holding your camera.

USE MOTION-STOPPING SHUTTER SPEEDS

If the camera, the subject, or both should move during a relatively long exposure, the film will record a blurred image. To record a sharp, clear image, you need a shutter speed fast enough to freeze such motion. Shutter-priority automatic cameras pose no problem in this regard, as you select the shutter speed and the camera selects the lens opening. With an aperture-priority camera, you select the lens opening and the camera selects the shutter speed. You can compel an aperture-priority camera to select the highest possible shutter speed for the circumstances by choosing the largest lens opening that does not require a shutter speed faster than the camera's top shutter speed. Monitor the camera's exposure readouts to be sure. The only way to induce a programmed automatic camera, which sets both the shutter speed and the lens opening, to use a relatively rapid shutter speed in low light is to use fast film.

STOPPING CAMERA MOTION

There is a useful rule of thumb for estimating the slowest shutter speed you are likely to be able to use successfully in handheld photography. Place the number 1 above the focal length of the camera lens expressed in millimetres and consider the resulting fraction as the slowest shutter speed to use with that lens when you are handholding the camera. For example, with a 35 mm wide-angle lens, the equivalent shutter speed would be 1/35 second. In fact, 1/30 second is the closest marked shutter speed found on modern cameras, and that would be the base shutter speed with that lens.

Slowest Shutter Speed for Handholding a Camera—Average Conditions

$$\frac{1}{\text{Lens Focal Length in Millimetres}} \text{ Second}$$

You can test your ability to hold a camera steady by shining a beam of light in a darkened room at a small mirror taped to your camera at about 45° to the lens axis. If the patch of light the mirror

People differ in their ability to hold a camera steady, and a particular person's ability can change quite a bit, depending on what he or she has been doing prior to photography. When you are well rested and calm, you may be able to handhold a camera at somewhat slower shutter speeds than the formula suggests. When you are tired, have run up several flights of stairs and are being buffeted by revelers or a stiff breeze, considerably faster shutter speeds would be advisable. Bear in mind, too, that the formula does not take into account stopping subject motion, nor does it allow for the beneficial effects of bracing yourself and/or the camera.

As a practical matter, many photographers find that they can also obtain satisfactory results at 1/30 second with a normal focal-length lens under favorable circumstances. Equally as practical, use faster than minimum shutter speeds whenever conditions permit and depth of field is not an important consideration.

Be especially watchful to use high enough shutter speeds with telephoto lenses and zoom lenses at telephoto settings. These lenses magnify the effects of camera motion as well as the image of the subject. To add to the difficulty in using these lenses for existing-light photography, they are usually longer, larger, and heavier, than normal focal-length and wide-angle lenses. This results in a more unwieldy camera-lens combination that is harder to hold steady. Use a shutter speed at least as high as the rule states or a shutter speed one or more steps higher when possible.

reflects moves noticeably when you trip the shutter, keep practicing to develop a gentler touch on the shutter release button and a steadier camera-holding technique.

John Menihan. Jr.

Neil Montanus

To capture active subjects sharply, select shutter speeds fast enough to stop the action. Very high-speed films, such as KODACOLOR VR 1000 Film which was exposed for 1/1000 second at f/2.8 to make this picture, are the most practical choices for photographing moving subjects.

If you cannot use as high a shutter speed as necessary to stop the action, wait to take the picture until a peak in the action occurs. Here the photographer waited until the diver was at the peak of her dive before making the exposure at 1/125 second.

STOPPING SUBJECT MOTION

With active subjects, use the highest shutter speeds you can to stop motion in your pictures. To do so in any but the brightest existing-light situations requires the use of high-speed films and large lens apertures. The table on the next page indicates shutter speeds recommended to stop various types of motion at different distances from the camera and assumes different directions of travel relative to the lens axis and film plane.

Quite often, existing light will not be bright enough to allow using as high a shutter speed as you would like. There are two basic and opposite ways to stop action in photos. The first is to wait until there is a lull in the action or a peak moment when the moving element appears suspended or slowed for an instant, and can be stopped effectively in pictures at a slower shutter speed. The other approach is to pan the camera with the moving subject.

SHUTTER SPEEDS FOR STOPPING ACTION   For Normal Focal-Length Lenses

Speed of Subject Motion		Moving Subject	Distance from Camera		Direction of Subject Motion		
Miles Per Hour	Kilometres Per Hour		Feet	Metres	← OR →	↖↗ OR ↙↘	↑ OR ↓
					Shutter Speed in Seconds		
5	8	**Slow Action**—People walking, children playing with moderate motion, babies not holding still	12 25 50 100	4 8 15 30	1/500 1/250 1/125 1/60	1/250 1/125 1/60 1/30	1/125 1/60 1/30 1/15
10	16	**Moderately Fast Action**—Children running, horses moving at a moderate pace; baseball, football, soccer, and hockey players moving at a medium pace; boxers, wrestlers, gymnasts, bowlers, parades, slow-moving vehicles, amusement park rides, performers, skaters, swimmers	12 25 50 100	4 8 15 30	1/1000 1/500 1/250 1/125	1/500 1/250 1/125 1/60	1/250 1/125 1/60 1/30
25	40	**Fast Action**—Fast runners, running horses, divers; basketball players, baseball, football, soccer, and hockey players moving at a fast pace; fast moving skaters, moving cars in traffic	12 25 50 100	4 8 15 30	1/2000 1/1000 1/500 1/250	1/1000 1/500 1/250 1/125	1/500 1/250 1/125 1/60
50	80	**Very Fast Action**—Race cars, motorcycles, race horses; field and track events with rapid motion; tennis players	25 50 100 200	8 15 30 61	1/2000 1/1000 1/500 1/250	1/1000 1/500 1/250 1/125	1/500 1/250 1/125 1/60

Note: You can estimate in-between values in the table.

This table indicates shutter speeds that will allow stopping the action of various moving subjects sharply when using a normal focal-length lens. With a wide-angle lens of about half the focal length of the normal lens, you can use the next slower shutter speed. With a telephoto lens of about double the focal length of the normal lens, use the next faster shutter speed.

Sports photographers often resort to panning the camera to record fast moving subjects reasonably sharp at slower-than-optimum shutter speeds. Here, panning during an exposure of 1/30 second at f/4 on KODACOLOR VR 1000 Film recorded the moving subject distinctly while blurring the background giving the photograph a look of action and speed.

Panning

Panning means tracking the moving subject by swinging the camera smoothly to keep the subject in a particular spot in the viewfinder, and continuing to move the camera to follow the subject during the exposure. Panning lets you make sharp pictures of rapidly moving subjects at surprisingly slow shutter speeds, and is much practiced by sports photographers. Stationary objects or those moving opposite the direction of camera motion will be blurred, adding to the impression of speed. The most important thing to remember when using the technique is to keep the camera moving with the subject throughout the exposure. Follow through briefly with the panning motion even after you hear the shutter click to be sure.

Bruce Nett

DEPTH OF FIELD

Depth of field refers to the zone of apparent sharpness that extends ahead of and behind the subject plane upon which you have focused. The greater the depth of field, the more objects in the field of view from near to far will appear to be rendered sharply on film. The more limited the depth of field, the fewer objects outside the plane of exact focus will appear to be rendered sharply. Depth of field is governed by three photographic factors: lens aperture, distance from the subject, and focal length of the lens. When the subject distance remains unchanged, depth of field and image size are controlled by the aperture and the focal length of the camera lens.

Other factors remaining constant, the smaller the lens aperture, the more depth of field you obtain. In a given situation, a very wide aperture such as $f/1.4$ or $f/2$ yields minimal depth of field whereas a small aperture such as $f/11$ or $f/16$ produces much greater sharpness in depth of field.

For any given lens aperture, depth of field increases as the image size on the film decreases and the depth of field decreases as image size increases. The image size becomes smaller when you use a shorter focal length lens and/or move farther from the subject. Image size becomes larger when you use a longer focal length lens and/or move closer to the subject.

With a specific focal-length lens set to a given aperture, the closer the focusing distance the less depth of field you will obtain and the greater the focusing distance the greater the depth of field.

When the aperture and subject distance remain constant, depth of field increases as focal length of the lens decreases and depth of field decreases as the focal length increases. For example, if you are photographing with a wide-angle-to-telephoto zoom lens with the aperture set to $f/4$ while maintaining a fixed distance from the subject, changing the zoom setting to change image size and the focal length will also change depth of field. At wide-angle settings, which produce small image size, depth of field will be comparatively great. At longer focal lengths at the same subject distance, which yield larger image sizes on film, depth of field will decrease noticeably.

Both pictures were made with the same camera and lens at the same distance from the subject. In the picture at left, made at $f/2$, only the subject is sharp. The shallow depth of field rendered foreground and background details as blurs. The picture at right was made with the aperture set to $f/11$. The greater depth of field obtained at the smaller aperture rendered foreground and background areas more sharply. KODAK EKTACHROME 200 Film (Daylight).

The same camera and lens were used to make both of these pictures, with the lens set at $f/5.6$ for both photos. In the picture made at close range, there is little depth of field despite the moderate aperture. Increasing the distance increased the depth of field significantly even though the aperture remained the same. KODACOLOR VR 200 Film, 1/125 second.

Both of these photographs were made with the same camera and wide-angle-to-telephoto zoom lens at the same distance. The lens was set at f/4 for both pictures. In the photo made at the 35 mm wide-angle setting, which yields a comparatively small image size on film, more depth of field is evident than in the picture made at the 105 mm telephoto setting, which produces a larger image. KODAK EKTACHROME 200 Film (Daylight), 1/30 second.

Depth of Field in Low Light

Any time you anticipate a need to stop motion without sacrificing depth of field in an existing-light situation, reach for the highest-speed film available, and if necessary, consider push processing it an additional stop when possible. In low light, when action-stopping and good depth of field are both required, there is simply no substitute for film speed.

When depth of field is important and there is little or no subject motion, use a tripod or other firm camera support. Then you can use slower shutter speeds in conjunction with smaller lens apertures to obtain the depth of field you need.

If you use an SLR camera that allows previewing depth of field, check the depth of field at the actual shooting aperture. Or, refer to the depth-of-field scale on the lens, if there is one, as explained in the owner's manual accompanying the camera or lens. If there's no depth-of-field scale on the lens, there may be one included in the instruction manual. In many existing-light situations, particularly those with a journalistic flavor, limited depth of field may actually enhance the effect of the picture and look more convincing than unexpected sharpness from foreground to background.

When conditions don't allow stopping motion and obtaining great depth of field simultaneously, you will rarely be wrong if you opt to stop motion. A picture in which only the subject appears sharp is preferable to one in which everything but the subject appears sharp or in which nothing at all is sharp.

If you need increased depth of field and don't have to worry about subject movement, put your camera on a tripod or other steady support. Then you can use slow shutter speeds with the lens set to smaller apertures. KODAK EKTACHROME 200 Film (Daylight), 1/4 second between f/5.6 and f/8.

Sometimes journalistic or candid subjects look more natural and convincing when depicted with limited depth of field. And shallow depth of field helps rivet the viewer's attention on the subject, softening irrelevant details in the foreground and/or background. KODAK TRI-X Pan Film, 1/60 second f/2, normal focal length lens.

FOCUS CAREFULLY

Because of the limited depth of field associated with the large lens apertures required for many existing-light situations, it behooves you to focus carefully on the primary subject. At wide apertures, there may not be much margin for error. This is especially important at close shooting distances and with telephoto lenses.

At very close range, you may find it easier to focus by moving the camera nearer to or farther from the subject than by adjusting the focusing ring. Once you've achieved proper focus, be careful to maintain it. Don't bend closer or lean back because even a slight distance change may exceed the available depth of field at a large lens aperture, and the subject may be somewhat soft, or out of focus. Conversely, if the subject moves even a little closer to or farther from the camera, refocus.

With zoom lenses you can focus more accurately if you focus with the lens set to the maximum focal length and then adjust the lens to the focal length you want to use for taking the picture. Focusing is most critical at the longest focal length for the lens. You can use this technique only with zoom lenses that do not change focus when the zoom focal-length setting is changed, not with varifocal lenses which do change focus.

When you must choose between stopping action and obtaining more depth of field, you are safer using the higher shutter speed rather than the smaller aperture. Sacrificing shutter speed to increase depth of field can result in an action picture in which the subjects are not sharp. KODACOLOR VR 1000 Film, 1/125 second f/4 (left), 1/500 second f/2 (right).

Automatic Focusing

If your camera features automatic focusing, read the owner's manual carefully to determine whether or not you must take any special precautions or follow different procedures when photographing in dim light. Some auto-focus systems lose efficiency in low light. If that is the case, or you suspect it might be, override the automatic system or switch it off and focus manually, if possible.

To insure accurate focusing, take care that the auto-focus mechanism responds to the principal subject or another feature at the same distance from the camera. If the auto-focus system "reads" a target closer or farther than the subject, it will set the focus for that target rather than for the subject. This can occur easily in busy interiors if the subject is not close enough to dominate the auto-focus system, which may then set focus for a prominent piece of furniture, a room divider, or a potted palm. Erroneous focus

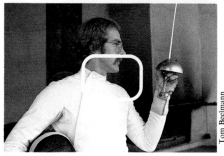

Asymmetrical compositions like this (left, top) often make for more interesting pictures but can trick autofocus systems into setting focus for features other than the principal subject. If the main subject is outside of the focus area indicated in the viewfinder, focus manually. Or, if the camera has a focus hold, frame the subject centrally while the camera focuses; then lock the focus setting while reframing the scene as desired. See your camera manual.

27

settings can also occur when you compose a picture asymmetrically, with the subject off-center. In conditions that are likely to trick an auto-focus system, focus manually if possible. Or if the camera has a focus hold, aim the camera precisely with the principal subject centered in the indicated focus area in the viewfinder for optimum focusing accuracy, then use the focusing lock to hold the focus setting while you reframe the scene for the desired composition.

KEEP YOUR LENSES CLEAN

Clean lenses are a must in existing-light photography because the scenes often include fairly bright lights in the picture field, frequently as main subject elements. So keep your lenses clean to reduce the likelihood of recording undesirable flare effects and image degradation that can be caused by particles of dust and dirt reflecting and refracting light unpredictably. These detrimental effects can prevent recording existing-light subjects sharply.

MAKING LONG EXPOSURES

Sometimes you can only create the pictures you want by making long exposures that do not permit handholding your camera. Perhaps you want to maximize depth of field or enjoy the extra-sharp, fine-grain rendition provided by a medium- or low-speed film. Nearly always, long exposures require using a tripod or other firm camera support to eliminate camera movement.

Certain types of subjects, like fireworks, are best photographed with long exposures to record the beauty of the display. Other subjects, such as moving car traffic and amusement park rides at night, create interesting streaks of light that portray motion when you use long exposure times. These techniques are described more fully in the chapter on "Existing-Light Photography in Public Places."

When you use long exposure times, you should be aware that some film characteristics can change. These effects are discussed on pages 61 and 66.

Using a Tripod

Setting up a tripod properly is usually easy and self-evident. Here are some tips you'll find useful.

For use on a level, flat surface, hold the tripod vertically at the appropriate height with the legs close together and touching the floor. Then adjust and lock the legs for the right length.

Set It Up Level

When erecting the tripod initially, adjust the length of individual legs as necessary so that the center column will be vertical and the top of the main section level. On a sloping or irregular surface you'll need to adjust the legs to different lengths to level the camera. You can make fine adjustments for framing with the tripod ball or pan head.

When the surface is flat and level you can adjust all three legs to the same length by holding the tripod straight up and down with the legs close together, touching the floor. Loosen the leg locking mechanisms and adjust the length of the legs by holding the tripod at the proper height. Lock one of the legs to the proper length. Then with the tripod vertical, all three legs resting on the floor, and the tripod's weight supported by the leg that's locked, lock the length of the other two legs to the same length as the first one.

Use a Wide Base for Stability

Always spread the tripod legs fully unless space limitations prevent doing so. The wider the base, the more stable the setup.

Adjust Leg Length for Camera Height

Insofar as possible, establish camera height by extending the tripod legs rather than the center column. Extending the legs makes the setup more stable. Raising the column excessively makes it more tippy. Raise the center column only for minor height adjustments. When you don't need the full height of the tripod, extend the thicker portions of the legs first, and as little of the thinner portions of the legs as necessary, for a firmer tripod.

Lock All Settings

Use the clamps or lock rings provided to lock all adjustments securely. The tripod will be more rigid and the camera won't sag or creep out of position. Don't operate locking devices too forcefully, though, particularly rotating collars, or they may freeze into position and require the use of tools to unlock. And keep locking mechanisms clean and free of grit or sand, which accelerate wear and can cause jamming.

Attach the Camera with Care

When engaging the tripod's mounting screw in the camera's tripod socket, stop turning the screw when it is just barely finger-tight. Forcing the screw deeper than it should go can cause serious internal damage to the camera as well as external blemishes.

Shake-Free Exposures

For consistently sharp exposures with a tripod-mounted camera, use a cable release to trip the shutter. If the camera rests on an improvised support and you don't have a cable release with you, hold the camera in place firmly with one hand while gently pressing the shutter release with the other. If the subject is immobile, you can also use the self-timer, if your camera has one, to release the shutter without jarring the camera.

Some SLR cameras have a mirror release that lets you swing the reflex mirror out of the light path. Then you can stop down the lens to taking aperture before tripping the shutter. If your camera is so equipped, actuate the control several seconds before initiating the exposure so any mechanical vibrations will dissipate before the shutter opens.

The techniques for making better existing-light pictures outlined in this chapter can be learned easily with a little practice. The best way to practice them is in the course of your everyday picture-taking. Just as they improve results when photographing by existing light, so they will improve the pictures you make under less challenging conditions.

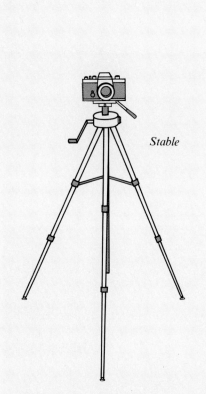
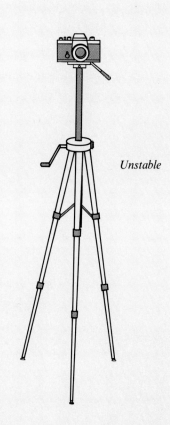

Stable

Unstable

When you use a tripod, spread the legs fully to create a broad, stable footing (left). Don't spread them partially (right) unless you are in a cramped area that doesn't permit full deployment. Position the camera at the height you prefer by extending the tripod legs, and use the center column for minor adjustments (left). Raising the center column excessively (right) decreases stability.

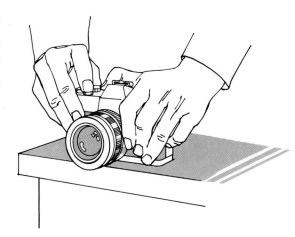

To trip the shutter with minimal vibration when you don't have a cable release, press the camera firmly against a steady support with one hand while pressing the shutter button gently. You can use this technique with the camera on an improvised support as shown or when it's on a tripod.

Determining Exposure

DETERMINING EXPOSURE FOR EXISTING-LIGHT SUBJECTS

Differences between existing light and familiar outdoor daylight conditions are reflected in methods used to determine exposure. Existing light is nearly always dimmer. It is frequently less evenly distributed. It may come from several different sources and directions simultaneously. And the light sources themselves are sometimes the subjects of existing-light photographs. Although the basic principles of determining existing-light exposure are the same as for daylight photography, you may have to apply them differently for best results.

The light sources themselves are sometimes the subjects of existing-light photographs.

Robert Brink

Existing light is nearly always dimmer than outdoor daylight. Unlike daylight, which emanates from a single source, existing light in a scene is often produced by multiple light sources.

John Vaeth

Caroline Grimes

Lighting in existing-light scenes is often uneven. But this usually helps make the photograph more dramatic and interesting.

Bruce Nett

Reflected-light meters tend to suggest exposure settings that render dark existing-light scenes too light on color-slide films (left). To retain the mood of the scene, underexpose 1/2 to 1 stop relative to the exposure indicated by the meter reading. Here, a 1-stop reduction in exposure restored the mood and appearance of the original scene (right). KODAK EKTACHROME 160 Film (Tungsten).

Proper Exposure in Existing Light

The conventional concept of proper exposure assumes that the film should be sufficiently exposed by image-forming light to depict the subject in a familiar and realistic way. That is, light subject tones should look light in the picture, medium tones should look medium, and dark tones should look dark. These criteria apply, too, in many existing-light situations, but with some important exceptions.

To record dim existing-light scenes so that they retain on film the dark quality and mood that characterize them in reality may require underexposing them by approximately 1/2 to 1 stop relative to the exposure suggested by a reflected-light meter. This is important to remember when using color-slide films because the film exposed in the camera becomes the final picture with no opportunity to alter the rendition in an intermediate step, such as printing. Prints from color and black-and-white negative films can be darkened to the desired degree during printing unless grossly overexposed. This may require custom printing or printing in your own darkroom to get the results you want.

If you follow the meter reading exactly, the exposure effect may not be readily apparent because slightly overexposed slides of dark scenes may appear normal and appear to have correct exposure. These slides are usually acceptable, but are too light compared with the actual appearance of the scene. This happens because exposure meters tend to make the brightness of tones in the scene appear average in photographs regardless of their actual brightness. This exposure effect is more easily overlooked with dark scenes when there are no lights in the pictures to serve as references as to how bright or dim the original scenes actually appeared.

When photographing night scenes outdoors, avoid inadvertent overexposure that might turn night into day on film. This can happen easily if your light meter reads a large expanse of dark background and proceeds to give you information aimed at rendering it several shades lighter. This effect will be explained more fully in the following discussion of exposure meters.

Underexposure causes lack of detail in shadow areas. Color and black-and-

white negatives will be too light, or thin, and color negatives will have increased graininess. Prints from underexposed negatives will have milky, gray shadows, flat contrast, and an overall muddy appearance. Underexposed color slides will be too dark.

Overexposure causes loss of definition, and with black-and-white negatives, increased graininess. Negatives will be darker and harder to print. Overexposed color slides will be too light with desaturated colors and loss of detail in highlight areas.

Setting aside for a moment conventional criteria for proper exposure, it can be helpful to define proper exposure for existing-light photography as the degree of exposure that produces an image that appears realistic or looks the way you want it to look. How you want it to look is your decision. How you can make it look that way is discussed in the balance of this chapter.

Don Chamberlin

Overexposing a night scene outdoors can turn it almost into an odd-looking daytime scene. Don't let a reflected-light meter read too much of the dark surroundings or the black night sky or it will encourage overexposure. This picture was taken by moonlight. To make a picture lighted by the full moon look like it was taken in daylight, try an exposure of 90 seconds at f/2 on KODAK EKTACHROME 400 Film (Daylight).

EXPOSURE METERS

To expose film properly, you have to relate the brightness of light reflected from the subject toward the camera or the brightness of the light illuminating the subject to the sensitivity of the film you are using. Exposure meters, or light meters, are sensing devices that do that and express the relationship in terms of shutter speeds and *f*-stops. Because the human eye is not good at quantifying light, exposure meters are almost indispensable to most existing-light photography. To make most effective use of exposure meters, it helps to understand how they work.

Reflected-Light Exposure Meters

All exposure meters built into cameras and many handheld meters measure the brightness of light reflected from the subject and are therefore known as reflected-light meters. The discussions concerning reflected-light exposure meters in this book apply both to separate handheld exposure meters and in-camera meters. The exposure information a reflected-light meter provides is influenced by both the illumination level of the light source and the reflective properties of the subject. It will advise less exposure for a subject that reflects much light and more exposure for a subject that reflects little light, even if the two subjects are side by side and identically illuminated. Thus, reflected-light meters tend to suggest camera settings that somewhat overexpose extremely dark subjects and underexpose predominantly light subjects. As mentioned earlier, this happens because these meters tend to make all subjects appear average in brightness—the brightness equivalent to medium gray—in pictures.

A reflected-light meter measures the brightness of light reflected from the subject. The reflective properties of the subject, as well as the overall light level, will influence the meter reading. Aim your meter at the subject from the same direction as the camera to measure the light reflected from the subject toward the camera. This procedure also applies to in-camera meters.

Incident-Light Exposure Meters

Some handheld exposure meters are designed to read the brightness of the light falling on the subject, known as incident light. Incident-light meters do not consider the actual reflective qualities of the subject at all but consider that everything has a reflectance equivalent to medium gray. In a constant light level, an incident-light meter will suggest the same exposure for a coat of black velvet as for a dress of white lace. Incident-light meters therefore tend to suggest camera settings that may slightly underexpose unusually dark subjects or overexpose extremely light ones.

An incident-light meter measures the brightness of light illuminating the subject. Its reading is not affected by the subject's reflective properties. To use an incident-light meter, you position it near the subject with the light-sensitive cell pointed toward the camera in order to measure the light illuminating the side of the subject you want to photograph.

An average, typically lighted indoor scene contains a distribution of light and dark and bright and dim elements that average medium gray.

Robert Clemens

The World as Exposure Meters "Think They See It"

Both reflected- and incident-light exposure meters are designed with the same underlying assumption that most subjects, most of the time, are of average tone and reflectance. The average indoor scene has a reflectance equal to a medium gray of 18 percent. This is the reasoning behind neutral gray cards, such as KODAK *Gray Cards*, R-27 which have 18 percent reflectance, sometimes used as a substitute from which to obtain an average exposure-meter reading. These 8 x 10-inch cards are sold by photo dealers and include instructions for use.

Reflected-light meters assume that you are pointing them at a medium-gray world, so their exposure recommendations for the subject they measure will record it on film as a medium gray or an equivalent brightness in color. This will help you in your visualization of how the exposure will appear on the film. Normal exposure meter readings are fine for average tone subjects because they usually should be recorded on film as medium-tone brightnesses. But if your meter mainly measures a bright area or a dark area in the scene, the indicated exposure will also make that area appear as a medium-tone brightness in the picture and will result in incorrect exposure. These situations require exposure adjustments to obtain correct exposure.

Many existing-light scenes, especially those outdoors at night, are predominantly darker than an average subject. When a reflected-light meter reads such a scene, the exposure settings indicated by the meter will produce overexposure in an attempt to make the scene appear equivalent in brightness to medium gray on film. When you meter scenes that are darker than usual with a reflected-light meter, adjust the exposure settings to give about 1/2 to 1 full stop less exposure than the meter recommends to avoid rendering the scene lighter than it looks.

Conversely, if the subject is an unusually light element in the scene or is actually the light sources themselves, a reflected-light meter reading of the light areas will provide exposure information to record them, too, as a brightness equivalent to medium gray by underexposing them. To avoid overly dark rendition, set the camera for approximately 1/2 to 1 stop more exposure than the meter indicates.

Caroline Grimes

If the subject is unusually light, increase the exposure indicated by a reflected-light meter by 1/2 to 1 stop. KODAK EKTACHROME 160 Film (Tungsten) with ESP-1 Processing.

Tom Beelmann

When photographing light sources, an exposure based on a reflected-light reading directly from the light sources will look darker and more saturated in color than the lights looked in reality. An additional 1/2 or 1 stop more exposure beyond the meter indication will usually lighten the rendition to approximate the visual appearance. Here a full stop of additional exposure brightened the lights. KODAK EKTACHROME 160 Film (Tungsten), 1/30 second between f/4 and f/5.6.

An incident-light meter measures only the intensity of the light falling on it and indicates a standard exposure setting that assumes a subject of normal brightness characteristics. With an average subject in a generally dark existing-light locale, the basic reading will yield an exposure level that records the scene much as it looks to your eye because the meter makes no attempt to "correct" for the dark areas surrounding the subject. You generally don't have to fudge the meter reading to preserve the mood of the scene with average subjects in lighter-than-average surroundings either with an incident meter, provided you want the photo to look light, as the scene appeared.

When the subject itself, not the surroundings or the illumination, is lighter than average, it will record lighter and

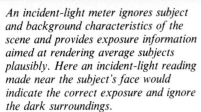

*An incident-light meter ignores subject
and background characteristics of the
scene and provides exposure information
aimed at rendering average subjects
plausibly. Here an incident-light reading
made near the subject's face would
indicate the correct exposure and ignore
the dark surroundings.*
*Courtesy Scholastic/KODAK Photography Awards

Harold W. Pique, SKPA*

John Fish

Lee Howick

when the subject is darker than average,
it will record darker if you take an incident-light meter reading at face value.
Most of the time the rendition will be appropriate when the subject is only somewhat lighter or darker than average.
However, when the subject is much
lighter or darker than average, you
should alter the exposure indicated by an
incident-light meter. For unusually light
subjects, decrease exposure 1/2 to 1 stop;
for unusually dark subjects, increase exposure 1/2 to 1 stop. Note that these corrections are just the opposite of those
required for a reflected-light meter.

An important exception when using an
incident-light meter, though, involves
photographing light sources. Here an incident meter is of little help, as it cannot
correctly measure the light source directly. For photographing light sources,
you're better off determining exposure
with a reflected-light meter or an exposure table.

*When performers are lighted by spotlights
with a dark surround, an averaging
reflected-light exposure meter would read
too much dark background and
overexpose the performers. Conversely,
when a subject is backlighted by window
light, an averaging meter would be fooled
by the bright background into reacting as
if the whole scene was lighter than usual*

*and underexpose the subject. A reflected-
light spot meter would help achieve
correct exposure by limiting the metered
area to significant parts of the subject,
while ignoring the irrelevant background.
You can obtain similar selectivity with an
averaging meter when conditions permit
you to approach the subject for a close-up
reading.*

34

Exposure Meter Coverage

Reflected-light meters, like lenses, have a wide or narrow angle of view. Meters that read a fairly wide angle of view are called averaging meters. They present exposure data based on the average of light and dark areas in the scene being read. Most handheld meters and built-in light meters in cameras are averaging types. They are quick and easy to use and don't require much decision-making most of the time. If you use an averaging meter, remember that it will attempt to give more exposure than necessary when it reads a scene containing unusually large dark areas, such as a well lighted performer standing on an otherwise dark stage. The same meter would tend to underexpose the performer if the background were substantially lighter or brighter.

Narrow-angle reflected-light meters, as the term implies, have a restricted reading angle and you can aim them selectively at limited areas of the scene. Meters with extremely narrow reading angles are called spot meters. Spot meters and narrow-angle meters require more skill and judgment to use successfully, but reward the careful worker with precise exposure measurement. They are extremely useful for calculating exposure when a relatively small significant subject area appears against much lighter or darker surroundings. Spot meters are handy for existing-light theatrical and sports subjects, and for making meter readings directly from light sources when you want to photograph the lights themselves. They are somewhat slow to use well for general photography because you must be careful to read areas that are not atypically light or dark, or you may have to make a series of readings of different subject areas and then average them yourself to determine a reasonable overall exposure.

Some 35 mm SLR cameras incorporate center-weighted reflected-light metering systems that represent a compromise between averaging and spot meters. Center-weighted exposure meters typically read everything in the field of view of the lens, but are more influenced by the central portion of the field than by the edges. When using a center-weighted meter, determine exposure with the subject of prime importance centered in the

A sensitive exposure meter is desirable for calculating exposure in low light, although you can often manage well by referring to an exposure table if a scene is too dim for your meter to respond or is not suitable for making a meter reading.

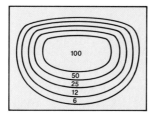

Center-weighted, reflected-light exposure meter systems offer a compromise between spot and averaging systems. Major reading emphasis is placed on the central portion of the field because the principal subject is usually in that location in the frame, but outer regions also influence the exposure recommendation. The numbers indicate percentages of sensitivity.

meter field which is usually the center of the viewfinder (see your camera manual), then reframe the scene if necessary for best composition. With an automatic camera you may have to use an exposure-hold system or switch to manual mode to prevent the exposure from changing when you reframe the scene.

Exposure Meter Sensitivity

For existing-light photography, the term exposure meter sensitivity refers primarily to the basic ability to respond accurately to dim light. The more sensitive the meter is, the lower the light levels in which you can use it. Nearly all modern battery-powered exposure meters are capable of reading in light dim enough to require high-speed film for handheld photography. Some extremely sensitive meters can read easily in light so dim that you would have to use a tripod, high-speed film, and lengthy exposures to record a usable image. If your exposure meter doesn't respond adequately in low light, you can make a substitute reading from a piece of white paper or a white card to get a higher meter reading. See page 38 for how to compensate exposure for the higher meter reading. If this technique is impractical, you can still make good existing-light pictures by referring to exposure tables.

EXPOSURE UNDER EVEN ILLUMINATION

It's generally easy to determine exposure in even lighting because you don't have to be concerned with extremely bright and dark areas coexisting within the same frame of film. As long as the scene doesn't include unusually reflective or nonreflective subjects of major importance, you can take a general, average reading at the indicated value. Even lighting is especially helpful when your subject is moving about, because no matter where the subject goes, the exposure is likely to remain the same. To verify that even lighting is indeed even, make several exposure readings in succession of different parts of the scene. If they are all the same or within a stop or less of each other, the lighting is even enough for you to photograph freely with no further exposure concerns as long as the lighting doesn't change.

If you need more film speed than the ISO (ASA) speed of your film provides and the film is a type that may be push processed, you will be able to double the film speed number with a corresponding processing adjustment and still obtain excellent results in even lighting. See pages 62, 63, and 65.

EXPOSURE UNDER UNEVEN ILLUMINATION

Many existing-light scenes are characterized by uneven lighting that illuminates some parts of the photographic field brightly while leaving others quite dark. This often makes the picture more interesting and natural looking. There are several ways to deal with such scenes, depending on how you wish the picture to look.

Meter the Extremes

One way to determine exposure for uneven illumination is to make exposure meter readings in the most important areas and then use a midpoint exposure. Begin by making meter readings of the lightest and darkest important areas where you want to see detail to determine the number of *f*-stops separating them. Don't include in your sample unimportant areas, such as glaringly bright elements like light bulbs or pitch black shadows in which you would not normally expect to see some detail and texture.

An overall reading with an averaging exposure meter provides good exposure data for evenly lighted subjects, such as *this one, which has no prominent areas that are unusually light or dark. KODACOLOR VR 1000 Film.*

Bruce Nett

Calculating exposure for unevenly lighted scenes, such as this one, requires metering both light and dark areas, then interpreting the readings to produce a *picture that looks the way you want it to look. KODAK EKTACHROME 400 Film (Daylight).*

Caroline Grimes

With color-negative and color-slide films, you can obtain reasonable exposure if the overall range from lightest important area to darkest important area is 6 stops or less by setting the camera for the midpoint of the range. You can expose most black-and-white films at a midpoint setting when the range is 8 stops or less and get excellent results. Exposure determined this way will provide conventional scene rendition. Light areas will look light, medium-tone areas will be medium-toned, and dark areas will look dark in the picture. This assumes proper printing of negative films. Keep in mind, though, that many scenes exceed the exposure ranges given here and frequently look good in photographs made at the midpoint exposure. The reason for this usually is that the midpoint exposure is good for the main subject, and viewers don't expect to see detail in deep shadows or brilliant highlights near light sources.

Decide What Matters Most

If you wish to produce a picture that is more an interpretation than a standard rendition, or if the metered range in a given situation exceeds the limits of the film you are using, you will need to make some decisions. First decide what you wish to show most clearly, such as the main subject, and make a meter reading of that area. Then set your camera for an exposure that will show the area as you think best, keeping in mind that a normal exposure meter reading will make the metered area record on the film as a medium brightness.

Next, consider the effect that exposure setting will have on lighter and darker areas that will also appear in the picture. If you are likely to record large areas of over- or underexposed surroundings that should show detail and that will detract from the subject, change your point of view or shooting distance to exclude them from the frame. If bright lights in the picture area are a problem in a home, use a camera angle that excludes them or move them outside the camera field of view. You could also turn them off if necessary but that means lowering the light level. Usually when photographing in home lighting you need as much illumination as possible from the existing lighting. In addition, when the existing room lights are turned on at night, they make the lighting more even and natural in appearance.

When people are prominent in the scene, choose an exposure that favors good skin-tone rendition, unless you are striving for a special effect, such as a silhouette. Viewers are less tolerant of improper skin tone rendition than they are of other subject matter. Even though the picture on the bottom (above) shows good detail in the lamp, the picture on the top is obviously better because it shows better detail for the girl. KODAK EKTACHROME 160 Film (Tungsten)

In harsh, contrasty lighting, it is usually better to favor good highlight and mid-tone exposure, even if it means losing considerable detail in darker areas. Exposing for darker values often creates unacceptable overexposed bright areas, especially with color-slide films. KODAK EKTACHROME 160 Film (Tungsten), 1/8 second f/8.

As a rule, if people are prominent in the scene, expose for reasonable skin-tone rendition even if it means sacrificing other areas somewhat. Picture viewers are generally less tolerant regarding the appearance of human subjects than they are about discrepancies in the appearance of inanimate objects.

With lighting that is not only uneven but also harsh and contrasty, forget about trying to retain much detail and texture in darker areas. Exposing for significant highlights and middle tones and letting the rest of the picture go dark can produce stark, dramatic pictures. Exposing for darker areas in such cases usually leads to unacceptable overexposure of highlights which are usually more important than dark shadows. This is particularly true with color-slide films.

If you must push process the film to expose it at a higher film speed number in harsh lighting, bias exposure settings to favor skin tones and brighter parts of the scene. Push processing increases film contrast, which makes burned out highlights more likely if exposures are pegged to low values.

SUBSTITUTE EXPOSURE METER READINGS

When you're unsure what part of a scene is the most suitable area to measure with a reflected-light meter, or if you cannot get close enough to make a meter reading of a significant area properly, make a close-up reading of the palm of your hand and set the camera for 1 stop more exposure than the meter indicates. That exposure level will be suitable for scenes that are about average in distribution and intensity of light and dark and will be right for skin tone, too. For dark skin, use 1 stop additional exposure. Make sure your hand is lighted the same as the scene you're photographing, place your exposure meter or camera with built-in meter close enough to fill its field of view with your hand, and be careful not to cast shadows on your hand from the meter or camera or part of your body. Readings made this way are similar to readings made from a gray card and readings obtained with an incident-light meter.

Since the brightness of people's palms may vary to some extent from one person to another, it's desirable to check an exposure meter reading of your palm compared with a meter reading of a gray test

37

Bruce Nett

Harvey Harland

In very dim light you can sometimes get an adequate exposure meter reading from a white card even though the meter doesn't respond sufficiently to a direct reading of the subject. Divide the film speed by 5 and reset the calculator on your exposure meter or film-speed dial on your camera to the lower number for a white-card reading. The lower film-speed setting compensates for the white card's greater-than-average reflectivity. Reset your meter or camera to the normal film speed immediately after you are finished with the white card.

card of known reflectance. You can use the KODAK Gray Card mentioned on page 33 for this purpose. Just hold your palm and a KODAK Gray Card so they're both lighted the same way in even light. Normally, the meter reading of the palm of your hand should indicate 1 stop less exposure than the KODAK Gray Card. If the difference, for example, is only +1/2 stop for your palm, use this factor to adjust exposures based on meter readings of your hand.

You can also use the KODAK Gray Card for making substitute exposure meter readings, instead. See the instructions included with the cards.

In light too dim for your exposure meter to respond decisively, reset the film speed dial to 1/5 of the actual ISO (ASA) speed of the film you are using. Then aim the meter at a white card or sheet of white paper held so that it is illuminated like the subject. You can use the white reverse side of the KODAK Gray Card for this purpose. The white target reflects about 5 times as much light as an average subject, so may jog the meter into providing an adequate response for a reliable reading. Dividing the film speed by 5 compensates for the fact that the meter is reading 5 times more brightness than it normally would under the circumstances. As soon as you are through determining exposure by this method, reset the meter dial to the actual film speed of the film you are using or the meter will provide grossly inaccurate exposure recommendations for readings made normally.

With lighted areas and lights both prominent in the photograph, the best picture is usually one made at an exposure halfway between the exposure that is best for the lights and the exposure that is best for dimly lighted areas. KODACOLOR VR 1000 Film, 1/125 second f/4.

USING EXPOSURE METERS OUTDOORS AT NIGHT

Existing-light picture opportunities outdoors at night fall into three main subject categories: Those in which the subject consists of both lights and lighted areas; those in which the subject is lighted but is not a light source; and those in which the subject is one or more light sources.

Exposing for Lighted Areas That Include Lights

General exposure meter readings that include both the lighted areas and the lights that will appear in the picture provide a sound data base from which to improvise, providing there are not large dark areas that would cause the meter to indicate camera settings that would produce overexposure. If the scene is fairly evenly lighted and relatively small light sources will appear in the picture, and there are no large dark areas, expose at the meter recommendation. If there are large lights or large black areas in the scene you want to photograph, you should decide where

Kodak Stuttgart

to place visual emphasis in the picture and expose accordingly. If you expose for the lights, less bright areas will tend to be underexposed and will appear darker in the picture than they may have seemed in reality. If you opt for realistic rendition of the areas that are dimly lighted as opposed to the lights, the latter will be overexposed and will wash out to some extent. The specifics of the scene itself and your personal tastes will dictate the best exposure choice.

Usually a compromise exposure, based on close-up meter readings, that records some detail in both lighted areas and lights in the scene is the best choice. Fortunately, exposure for outdoor night scenes is not critical and more than one exposure is usually acceptable.

For scenes that are difficult to meter, such as those with large dark areas, you may obtain better exposure by following the exposure tables in this book. See page 42–43. If the exposure indicated by your exposure meter differs significantly from the exposure suggested in the table, take pictures at both camera settings, bracket, and choose the picture with the best exposure. This will help you gain experience for other similar situations.

Exposing for Lighted Subjects

You can make exposure meter readings of floodlighted buildings, monuments, and sports arenas as though they were ordinary daytime subjects if you take extra precautions. Make sure your exposure meter reads as much of the subject as possible and that it is not influenced excessively by light sources in its field of view or by unusually large dark areas surrounding the subject. Either aim your meter to exclude such irrelevant reference tones or make close-up readings.

Instead of close-up meter readings, you can use a spot meter to help save footsteps if you have one. With an SLR camera, you can read exposure through a telephoto lens to limit the meter's field of view, then switch to whatever focal length lens frames the scene best. You can also do this with a zoom lens just by changing the zoom setting to telephoto setting to take the meter reading.

If possible, exclude light sources that look like sizable bright spots from the frame when making the actual exposure, too, to avoid distracting hot spots in the picture. Often, though, the light sources are not distracting and add to the dramatic appearance of a night subject. Sometimes the glare is blocked by reflectors on the light sources. It's rewarding to experiment and photograph the subject from several viewpoints including and excluding light sources in different pictures. Then you can choose the best one.

When photographing outdoor night subjects and using an exposure meter, exclude large dark areas surrounding the subject to avoid deflated readings that can cause overexposure of the main subject. A good method is to make close-up meter readings of the subject so the meter does not measure the dark surroundings. Similarly where light sources are an integral and essential part of the scene when using a meter, exclude the lights which can cause inflated readings and underexposure. Again the solution is to make close-up readings.

When reading exposure for lights themselves, fill the meter field with the lights and exclude dark surroundings that might trick the meter into recommending overexposure. KODAK EKTACHROME 160 Film (Tungsten), 1/60 second f/4.

Exposure for Photographing Light Sources

When light sources themselves, such as colorful signs or decorative lights at an amusement park, are the primary subject, make exposure meter readings directly from the light sources and exclude as much of the dark surround as possible. If necessary, approach a cluster of typical lights closely enough to fill the meter's field of view or make a spot or telephoto lens reading to ensure concentration on the lights.

Taking the meter reading at face value will yield color slides with good color saturation for the colored lights and little perceptible detail in darker areas. Increasing the exposure 1 stop will brighten the lights producing less saturation and increase identifiable detail in darker areas. Decreasing the exposure 1 stop from the meter reading will further saturate the colors of the lights while rendering the rest of the scene even darker. Hedge your bets by shooting all three exposure variations, then pick the version you like best. You can also use these exposure guidelines for color and black-and-white

40

negative films to obtain proper exposure, but tone rendition is controlled to a large extent when the prints are made.

WHEN IN DOUBT, USE EXPOSURE BRACKETING

Bracketing exposure consists of taking one picture at the shutter speed and f-stop determined by your exposure meter or recommended in an exposure table, or your best estimate of what the situation requires, then taking additional pictures with more and less exposure. Bracketing is an indispensable adjunct to existing-light photography, both as insurance that you will produce acceptable pictures in unfamiliar and/or unorthodox circumstances and during your initial encounters with low-light subjects before you gain the confidence of repeated success. If you are slightly uncertain about the best exposure setting, bracket by ± 1 stop. If you are very uncertain, extend the bracketing range to ± 2 stops or more. For more subtle control, bracket in 1/2-stop increments. With color-negative and black-and-white negative films, which are generally more tolerant of overexposure than underexposure, bracket toward more rather than less exposure unless the scene clearly carries the risk of overexposure of important elements.

Usually, with color and black-and-white negative films, 1-stop exposure increments are appropriate because of the films' exposure latitude. Since color-slide films have less latitude, 1/2-stop increments are usually better for existing-light subjects.

USING EXPOSURE TABLES

Sometimes it is difficult or impossible to determine exposure positively with an exposure meter for reasons ranging from "I forgot to replace the dead meter battery" to "I haven't the faintest idea where to point it." That's where exposure tables come to the rescue. Exposure tables are guides listing suggested exposures with one or more films for a variety of existing-light or other photographic situations. The exposure data presented in such tables are derived from actual picture-taking by experienced photographers using properly functioning photographic equipment. Instructions supplied with some Kodak films most suited to existing-light photography include existing-light exposure tables. The exposure

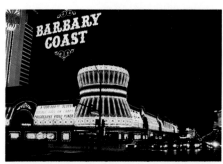

One stop more exposure, 1/60 second f/2

Normal exposure, 1/60 second f/2.8

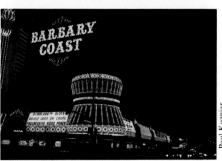

One stop less exposure, 1/60 second f/4

Bracketing consists of making several exposures of the same subject at different exposure settings. The examples above are 1 stop over the exposure indicated by the meter reading—more exposure; the normal exposure; and 1 stop under—less exposure. Think of bracketing as picture insurance. KODAK EKTACHROME 160 Film (Tungsten)

Caroline Grimes

table that closes this chapter presents data for existing-light exposures with a broad assortment of Kodak Films.

The information in exposure tables is sometimes included in dial-calculator exposure guides. The *KODAK Pocket Photoguide,* AR-21, sold by photo retailers, includes a convenient Existing-Light Exposure Dial for KODAK Films.

When you consult an exposure table, remember that the indicated exposures are for subjects and lighting conditions typical of the category and assume that equipment is in excellent operating condition. Because of possible subject and scene variations and anomalies in the performance of cameras and lenses, it's advisable to bracket your exposure for important pictures.

Besides their primary function of helping achieve proper exposure, these tables can play an important role in helping you learn to use an exposure meter well in existing light. Compare meter readings you make with the exposures recommended in the table. When they are the same or fairly similar, it's a sign that you're using your meter properly. If the settings your meter recommends differ significantly from those the table suggests, examine your metering technique because you may be doing something incorrectly. If your readings and the exposure table differ consistently with a variety of subjects and you are getting poor exposure, have your meter checked for accuracy and adjusted if necessary.

Exposure tables provide another helpful function, too—they're useful for planning purposes. The suggested exposures can help you select film and lenses with adequate speed to use for the kinds of subjects and lighting conditions you expect to encounter. Exposure tables for existing light may also suggest subject opportunities for pictures that had not occurred to you.

The more experience you acquire using exposure tables, the more you will appreciate how helpful these simple "paper exposure meters" can be.

Glassware in a window transilluminated by daylight is a subject that's difficult to read with an exposure meter for determining correct exposure because of the bright background. This is a situation where an exposure table can be helpful. Usually an exposure 1 stop greater than that required for the outdoor lighting gives good results. KODACHROME 64 Film (Daylight), 1/60 second f/8

SUGGESTED EXISTING-LIGHT EXPOSURES FOR *KODAK* FILMS

Picture Subject	KODACHROME 25 (Daylight)*† ISO (ASA) 25 / Technical Pan 2415* EI 25	KODACHROME 40 5070 (Type A)* ISO (ASA) 40 / PANATOMIC-X*† ISO (ASA) 32	KODACOLOR VR 100 ISO 100 / EKTACHROME 100 (Daylight)† ISO (ASA) 100 / KODACHROME 64 (Daylight)† ISO (ASA) 64	KODACOLOR VR 200 ISO 200 / EKTACHROME 200 (Daylight)† ISO (ASA) 200 / EKTACHROME 160 (Tungsten)† ISO (ASA) 160—normal processing / VERICHROME Pan ISO (ASA) 125 / PLUS-X Pan† ISO (ASA) 125	KODACOLOR VR 400, ISO 400 / EKTACHROME 400 (Daylight) ISO (ASA) 400—normal processing / EKTACHROME 200 (Daylight)† ISO (ASA) 400— / EKTACHROME 160 (Tungsten)† ISO (ASA) 320—ESP-1 Processing for 2 times normal film speed / TRI-X Pan, ISO (ASA) 400	KODACOLOR VR 1000 ISO 1000 / EKTACHROME P800/1600 Professional (Daylight) EI 800—ESP-1 Processing (Push 1) / EKTACHROME 400 (Daylight) ISO (ASA) 800—ESP-1 Processing for 2 times normal film speed	EKTACHROME P800/1600 Professional (Daylight) EI 1600 Push 2 Processing / 2475 Recording EI 1000 / ROYAL-X Pan ISO (ASA) 1250
AT HOME — Home interiors at night—Areas with average light / Areas with bright light	1/4 sec f/2	1/4 sec f/2 / 1/8 sec f/2	1/4 sec f/2.8 / 1/15 sec f/2	1/15 sec f/2 / 1/30 sec f/2	1/30 sec f/2 / 1/30 sec f/2.8	1/30 sec f/2.8 / 1/30 sec f/4	1/30 sec f/4 / 1/60 sec f/4
Candlelighted close-ups	—	—	1/4 sec f/2	1/8 sec f/2	1/15 sec f/2	1/30 sec f/2	1/30 sec f/2.8
OUTDOORS AT NIGHT — Indoor and outdoor holiday lighting at night / Christmas trees	1 sec f/2	1 sec f/2.8	1 sec f/4	1 sec f/5.6	1/15 sec f/2	1/30 sec f/2	1/30 sec f/2.8
Brightly lighted downtown street scenes (Wet streets add interesting reflections.)	1 sec f/5.6	1 sec f/2	1/30 sec f/2	1/30 sec f/2.8	1/60 sec f/2.8	1/60 sec f/4	1/125 sec f/4
Brightly lighted nightclub or theatre districts—Las Vegas or Times Square	1/15 sec f/2	1/15 sec f/2	1/30 sec f/2.8	1/30 sec f/4	1/60 sec f/4	1/125 sec f/4	1/125 sec f/5.6
Neon signs and other lighted signs	1/30 sec f/2	1/30 sec f/2	1/30 sec f/4	1/60 sec f/4	1/125 sec f/4	1/125 sec f/5.6	1/125 sec f/8
Store windows	1/15 sec f/2	1/30 sec f/2.8	1/30 sec f/4	1/30 sec f/4	1/60 sec f/4	1/60 sec f/5.6	1/60 sec f/8
Subjects lighted by street lights	—	—	1/4 sec f/2	1/8 sec f/2	1/15 sec f/2	1/30 sec f/2	1/30 sec f/2.8
Floodlighted buildings, fountains, monuments	1 sec f/2	1 sec f/2.8	1 sec f/4	1/2 sec f/4	1/15 sec f/2	1/30 sec f/2	1/30 sec f/2.8
Skyline—right after sunset	1/30 sec f/2.8	1/30 sec f/4	1/60 sec f/4	1/60 sec f/5.6	1/125 sec f/5.6	1/125 sec f/8	1/125 sec f/11
Skyline—10 minutes after sunset	1/30 sec f/2	1/30 sec f/2.8	1/30 sec f/4	1/60 sec f/4	1/60 sec f/5.6	1/125 sec f/5.6	1/125 sec f/8
Skyline—distant view of lighted buildings at night	8 sec f/2	4 sec f/2	4 sec f/2.8	1 sec f/2	1 sec f/2.8	1 sec f/4	1 sec f/5.6
Moving auto traffic on expressways—light patterns	20 sec f/8	20 sec f/11	20 sec f/16	10 sec f/16	10 sec f/22	10 sec f/32	5 sec f/32
Fairs, amusement parks	—	—	1/15 sec f/2	1/30 sec f/2	1/30 sec f/2.8	1/60 sec f/2.8	1/60 sec f/4
Amusement park rides—light patterns	4 sec f/8	4 sec f/11	4 sec f/16	2 sec f/16	1 sec f/16	1 sec f/22	—
Fireworks—displays on the ground	1/15 sec f/2	1/30 sec f/2	1/30 sec f/2.8	1/30 sec f/4	1/60 sec f/4	1/60 sec f/5.6	1/60 sec f/8
Fireworks—aerial displays (Keep shutter open on Bulb for several bursts.)	f/4	f/5.6	f/8	f/11	f/16	f/22	f/32*
Lightning (Keep shutter open on Bulb for one or two streaks of lightning.)	f/2.8	f/4	f/5.6	f/8	f/11	f/16	f/22
Burning buildings, campfires, bonfires	1/15 sec f/2	1/30 sec f/2	1/30 sec f/2.8	1/30 sec f/4	1/60 sec f/4	1/60 sec f/4	1/125 sec f/5.6
Subjects lighted by campfires, bonfires	—	—	1/8 sec f/2	1/15 sec f/2	1/30 sec f/2	1/30 sec f/2.8	1/30 sec f/4
Night football, soccer, baseball, racetracks‡	—	—	1/30 sec f/2.8	1/60 sec f/2.8	1/125 sec f/2.8	1/250 sec f/2.8	1/250 sec f/4
Niagara Falls—White lights / Light-colored lights / Dark-colored lights	15 sec f/2.8 / 30 sec f/2.8 / 30 sec f/2	15 sec f/4 / 30 sec f/4 / 30 sec f/2.8	15 sec f/5.6 / 30 sec f/5.6 / 30 sec f/4	8 sec f/5.6 / 15 sec f/5.6 / 30 sec f/5.6	4 sec f/5.6 / 8 sec f/5.6 / 15 sec f/5.6	4 sec f/8 / 4 sec f/5.6 / 8 sec f/5.6	4 sec f/11 / 4 sec f/8 / 4 sec f/5.6
Moonlit§—Landscapes / Snow scenes	— / —	— / —	30 sec f/2 / 15 sec f/2	15 sec f/2 / 8 sec f/2	8 sec f/2 / 4 sec f/2	4 sec f/2 / 4 sec f/2.8	4 sec f/2.8 / 4 sec f/2.8
Sydney, Australia—Opera House / Sydney Harbour Bridge / El Alamein Memorial Fountain	1 sec f/2.8 / 1 sec f/2 / 4 sec f/2	1/2 sec f/2.8 / 1 sec f/2.8 / 4 sec f/2.8	1/4 sec f/2.8 / 1/2 sec f/2.8 / 1 sec f/2	1/15 sec f/2 / 1/4 sec f/2.8 / 1 sec f/2.8	1/30 sec f/2 / 1/15 sec f/2 / 1/2 sec f/2.8	1/30 sec f/2.8 / 1/15 sec f/2 / 1/4 sec f/2.8	1/30 sec f/4 / 1/30 sec f/2.8 / 1/15 sec f/2

42

SUGGESTED EXISTING-LIGHT EXPOSURES FOR *KODAK* FILMS Continued

	Subject	Col 1	Col 2	Col 3	Col 4	Col 5	Col 6
OUTDOORS AT NIGHT	Canada—Skyline-close view, Toronto, Ontario	4 sec f/2.8	1 sec f/2.8	1/2 sec f/2.8	1/4 sec f/2.8	1/15 sec f/2	1/30 sec f/2
	Château Frontenac, Quebec, Quebec	1 sec f/2	1/2 sec f/2.8	1/4 sec f/2.8	1/15 sec f/2.8	1/30 sec f/2	1/30 sec f/2.8
	Parliament Building, Victoria, British Columbia	1/2 sec f/2.8	1/4 sec f/2.8	1/30 sec f/2	1/30 sec f/2.8	1/30 sec f/4	1/30 sec f/4
	Copenhagen, Denmark—Town Hall Square	1 sec f/2	1/2 sec f/2	1/4 sec f/2.8	1/15 sec f/2.8	1/30 sec f/2	1/30 sec f/2.8
	Little Mermaid	4 sec f/2.8	1 sec f/2	1/2 sec f/2.8	1/4 sec f/2.8	1/15 sec f/2	1/30 sec f/2
	The Restaurant Nimb, Tivoli Gardens	1/2 sec f/2.8	1/4 sec f/2.8	1/30 sec f/2.8	1/30 sec f/2.8	1/30 sec f/4	1/60 sec f/4
	England—Trafalgar Square; Piccadilly Circus; Leicester Square; Regent Street and Oxford Street Christmas Lighting, London	1/4 sec f/2.8	1/30 sec f/2	1/30 sec f/2.8	1/60 sec f/2.8	1/60 sec f/4	1/60 sec f/5.6
	Golden Mile, Blackpool	1 sec f/2	1 sec f/2	1/4 sec f/2	1/15 sec f/2	1/30 sec f/2	1/30 sec f/2.8
	Paris, France—Eiffel Tower	1 sec f/2.8	1/4 sec f/2.8	1/4 sec f/2	1/15 sec f/2.8	1/30 sec f/2.8	1/30 sec f/4
	Arc de Triomphe	1/2 sec f/2.8	1/4 sec f/2.8	1/30 sec f/2.8	1/30 sec f/2.8	1/60 sec f/2.8	1/60 sec f/4
	West Germany—Dom Cathedral from Deutzer Ufer, Cologne; Rothenburg on the Tauber, Rothenburg; Heidelberg Castle, Heidelberg	1/2 sec f/2.8	1/4 sec f/2.8	1/30 sec f/2	1/30 sec f/2.8	1/60 sec f/2.8	1/60 sec f/4
	Rome, Italy—Esedra Fountain; Navona Fountain	1 sec f/2	1 sec f/2.8	1/4 sec f/2.8	1/15 sec f/2.8	1/30 sec f/2	1/30 sec f/2.8
	Roman Forum: Coloseum	8 sec f/2	4 sec f/2	1 sec f/2.8	1/2 sec f/2.8	1/2 sec f/2.8	1/4 sec f/2.8
	Tokyo, Japan—Ginza Street; Kabuki Theater	1/4 sec f/2.8	1/15 sec f/2	1/30 sec f/2.8	1/60 sec f/2.8	1/60 sec f/4	1/125 sec f/4
	Shinjuku Skyscrapers	1/2 sec f/2.8	1/4 sec f/2.8	1/30 sec f/2.8	1/30 sec f/2.8	1/30 sec f/4	1/60 sec f/4
	Mexico City, Mexico—Independence Monument; Virgin of Guadalupe Shrine Interior	1 sec f/2.8	1/2 sec f/2.8	1/15 sec f/2	1/30 sec f/2.8	1/30 sec f/2.8	1/30 sec f/2.8
INDOORS IN PUBLIC PLACES	Basketball, hockey, bowling**	—	1/30 sec f/2	1/60 sec f/2	1/125 sec f/2	1/125 sec f/2.8	1/250 sec f/2.8
	Boxing, wrestling**	—	1/60 sec f/2	1/125 sec f/2	1/250 sec f/2	1/250 sec f/2.8	1/250 sec f/4
	Stage shows—Average	—	1/15 sec f/2	1/30 sec f/2.8	1/60 sec f/2.8	1/125 sec f/2.8	1/125 sec f/5.6
	Bright	1/30 sec f/2	1/60 sec f/2	1/60 sec f/4	1/125 sec f/4	1/250 sec f/4	1/250 sec f/4
	Circuses—Floodlighted acts	—	1/30 sec f/2	1/30 sec f/2.8	1/60 sec f/2.8	1/125 sec f/2.8	1/250 sec f/5.6
	Spotlighted acts (carbon-arc)	1/30 sec f/2	1/60 sec f/2	1/60 sec f/2	1/60 sec f/2.8	1/125 sec f/2.8	1/250 sec f/5.6
	Ice shows—Floodlighted acts	—	1/30 sec f/2	1/60 sec f/2.8	1/125 sec f/2.8	1/250 sec f/2.8	1/250 sec f/4
	Spotlighted acts (carbon-arc)	1/30 sec f/2	1/60 sec f/2	1/125 sec f/2.8	1/250 sec f/2.8	1/250 sec f/4	1/250 sec f/5.6
	Interiors with bright fluorescent light††	1/15 sec f/2	1/30 sec f/2	1/30 sec f/4	1/60 sec f/4	1/60 sec f/5.6	1/60 sec f/8
	School—stage and auditorium	—	—	1/15 sec f/2	1/15 sec f/2	1/30 sec f/2.8	1/30 sec f/4
	Swimming pool—tungsten light indoors** (above water)	—	—	1/15 sec f/2	1/60 sec f/2	1/60 sec f/2.8	1/60 sec f/4
	Hospital nurseries	1/15 sec f/2	1/30 sec f/2	1/30 sec f/2.8	1/60 sec f/2.8	1/60 sec f/4	1/125 sec f/4
	Church interiors—tungsten light	1 sec f/4	1/15 sec f/5.6	1/15 sec f/2	1/30 sec f/2.8	1/60 sec f/2.8	1/30 sec f/4
	Stained-glass windows, daytime—photographed from inside	Use 3 stops more exposure than for the outdoor lighting conditions.					
	Glassware in windows, daytime—photographed from inside	Use 1 stop more exposure than for the outdoor lighting conditions.					

Note: The suggested exposures are approximate. For important pictures, bracket at least 1 stop on either side of the exposure in the table.

[ ] For color slides of these scenes, use tungsten or Type A film for the most natural rendition. You can also use daylight color film, but your slides will look yellow-red.

[ ] For color slides of these scenes, use daylight film. You can also use tungsten film with a No. 85B filter, or Type A film with a No. 85 filter over your camera lens. When you use either of these filters, give 1 stop more exposure than that recommended for daylight film in the table.

[ ] For color slides of these scenes, you can use daylight, tungsten, or Type A film. Daylight film will produce colors with a warmer, more yellowish look. Tungsten or Type A film produces colors with a colder, more bluish appearance.

[▓] For color prints you can take pictures with KODACOLOR Films of all the scenes listed in the tables and get acceptable color quality.

Use a tripod or other firm support for shutter speeds slower than 1/30 second.

*These lower speed films are most suitable for motionless subjects, like inanimate objects, with your camera on a tripod.

†These exposures also apply to the professional versions of these films.

‡When you want color slides and the lighting at these events is provided by Multi-Vapor lamps, you should get good results on daylight film. If the lighting is mercury-vapor, your slides will appear greenish. When the lighting is tungsten, you'll get better results using tungsten film. See page 56.
Lighting provided by Multi-Vapor or mercury vapor lamps—high-intensity discharge lamps—may cause uneven exposure in the picture or underexposure when you use shutter speeds higher than 1/125 second. This effect is unpredictable, and depends on the lighting installation.

§Exposures are for the full moon unobscured. Since the moon will move during the exposure, don't include it in the picture or it will be blurred.

¶If f/32 is not on your camera lens, use the next larger lens opening.

**When the lighting for these events is provided by tungsten lamps and you want color slides, you'll get better results by using tungsten film. If the lighting is Multi-Vapor, color rendition will be better on daylight film. See page 56.

††With fluorescent lighting, use shutter speeds longer than 1/60 second to obtain uniform and adequate exposure.

KODAK Films for Existing-Light Photography

Most of the color and black-and-white films Kodak manufactures for general use may be used successfully for existing-light photography, depending on specific circumstances. The tables that conclude this chapter list films well suited to photography in existing light and outlines their characteristics. The following comments and considerations will help you select the ones that will best help you realize your personal vision.

Otto Done

44

Bruce Nett

John Menihan, Jr.

DEFINITION

Although existing-light photographers are often tempted to emphasize film speed above other qualities when choosing films, other important characteristics should be considered, too, as they affect definition. Definition is a composite effect of several factors including graininess, resolving power, and sharpness. These characteristics are related to film speed in ways that make it necessary at times to seek a compromise that favors one characteristic at the expense of another. Generally, Kodak films provide their best definition when they're exposed correctly and processed according to recommendations.

Modern film technology is remarkable when you consider the superb films photographers have available today. The state of the art of combining very high speed, ISO 1000, with relatively fine grain and pleasing color rendition is exemplified by KODACOLOR VR 1000 Film. This is an excellent film for existing-light photography, especially when conditions are demanding, such as when photographing dimly lighted subjects, using a handheld camera in low light, photographing action, or using telephoto lenses.

When you don't have to contend with subject or camera movement, you can make pictures that exhibit very little graininess by using a low-speed, extremely fine-grain film. Slower films usually show less graininess than faster films. This picture was made on KODAK PANATOMIC-X Film, ISO (ASA) 32, exposed for 1/2 second at f/5.6 in a tripod-mounted camera.

Graininess

Graininess is the textured or sandy effect that becomes apparent especially when an image is enlarged considerably. If you routinely make very large prints or project slides to extreme sizes, you are quite aware of the differences that exist among films with regard to graininess. As a rule, the higher the film speed the more pronounced a film's graininess will be. Relatively low-speed films such as KODACHROME 40 Film 5070 (Type A), have extremely fine grain that is difficult to detect even under extreme magnification. Very high-speed films such as KODACOLOR VR 1000 and KODAK Recording 2475 Films reveal their grain texture at lower degrees of enlargement than slower films. Graininess also increases somewhat when film is push-processed to permit exposures at higher than standard film-speed numbers.

When you want to stop motion in low light, you have to use a high-speed film that yields pictures displaying greater graininess than lower speed films. This action picture was made on KODAK Recording Film 2475, speed 1000, exposed for 1/1000 second at f/2.8 in a handheld camera.

If you expect to enlarge the final image to a size that makes graininess noticeable, you should consider the trade-off between film speed and graininess. To minimize graininess, you may have to give up some film speed by using a film with less speed, and therefore give up some motion-stopping ability or depth of field. Conversely, if you place a premium on stopping motion, gaining depth of field, or working with a handheld camera, you may have to accept more graininess because you need a film with higher speed. There are no universal solutions to these photographic considerations. Decide how you want the finished picture to look and choose accordingly. Note that with prints, graininess is usually not a concern in standard-album size or smaller prints made from full-frame 35 mm negatives.

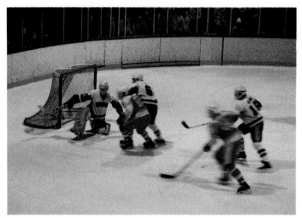

Bruce Nett

Norm Kerr

Here the photographer benefited from the inherent sharpness and extremely fine grain of KODACOLOR VR 100 Film when photographing an immobile subject. Supporting the camera on a tripod allowed using a slow shutter speed in conjunction with a moderate lens aperture that yielded sufficient depth of field.

Resolving Power and Sharpness

Resolving power refers to the ability of a film or print to record fine detail. Resolving power is usually expressed in lines per millimetre and is determined by photographing a high-contrast parallel-line test chart at great reductions in size. Descriptive adjectives, such as high, medium, or low, are assigned to various resolving power categories to make the measurements more meaningful in practical terms. See the Kodak film tables, pages 66–69.

In existing light, picture sharpness may depend more on film speed than on film sharpness and resolving power. The photograph at left was made on KODACOLOR VR 100 Film, which has very high sharpness and high resolving power, 1/30 second at f/2.8. The photograph at right was made on KODACOLOR VR 1000 Film, which has

Film sharpness refers to the precision with which a film records hard-edged subject contours—the boundaries separating detail that is dark in a photograph and detail that is light. As a rule, to which there are occasional exceptions, both resolving power and sharpness decrease somewhat as film speed increases.

Practically, when working in low light with a handheld camera, you are likely to produce sharper-looking pictures with high-speed films than with lower speed films, even though slower films may be inherently sharper, and have higher resolving power. The reason is that apparent picture sharpness is affected greatly by image motion and depth of field. The more completely image motion is stopped and the greater the depth of field, the sharper the picture looks, all other factors being equal. The faster the film in your camera, the more likely you are to stop motion successfully and to have adequate depth of field. On the other hand, when you plan to photograph immobile subjects with a tripod-mounted camera, don't overlook the lower speed films and their potential for producing breathtakingly sharp results.

medium sharpness and medium resolving power, so is inherently somewhat less sharp, 1/125 second at f/4. Nonetheless, the picture made on KODACOLOR VR 1000 Film looks sharper, because the much faster film allowed using a higher shutter speed for better action stopping and a smaller aperture for more depth of field.

KODAK COLOR NEGATIVE FILMS FOR COLOR PRINTS

Kodak color negative films, such as KODACOLOR VR 1000, KODACOLOR VR 400, KODACOLOR VR 200, and KODACOLOR VR 100 Films, record the subject in reversed tones and colors. The processed film's negative images are projected onto photographic paper to produce positive, full-color prints. You can also use color negatives to make color slides for projection as well as to make black-and-white prints. KODACOLOR Films are balanced for correct color rendition in light of daylight quality. However, you can also expose them with a wide variety of light sources and still produce attractive color rendition for noncritical applications, thanks to the opportunities for adjusting color when printing. When you require more precise color control, you can use suitable correction filters over the camera lens to match the color quality of image-forming light more closely to the daylight balance of the film. The relatively wide exposure latitude of color-negative films, particularly with regard to overexposure, helps them handle contrasty lighting with ease. They do not take kindly to underexposure, nor are they recommended for push processing.

Tom Beelmann

You can expose high-speed color negative films with many different light sources without corrective filtration because adequate color correction for noncritical use can be achieved when printing. These pictures were made on KODACOLOR VR 400 Film with ordinary household lamps. The photo on the top was taken with no filter on the camera lens at 1/30 second at f/5.6. Color was balanced in printing. The photo on the bottom was taken with a No. 80A conversion filter at 1/15 second at f/4. Less color adjustment was required in printing and the balance is more accurate, but this was achieved at the cost of a 2-stop reduction in film speed. For most uses, the top version would be equally acceptable, although less fully corrected. Usually it's not practical to use camera filters in existing light because of the necessity to increase exposure due to the light they absorb.

Some KODACOLOR VR Films now have electronic readable codes for potential use in future generations of 35 mm cameras. These codes will sense film speed, exposure latitude of the film, and number of exposures available, all automatically depending on the camera. The codes will be located on the film magazine, on a newly designed film leader, and along the edges of the film. Film cartons and magazines for the newly coded film will display the designation "DX," which will be identified by a special symbol. Eventually all popular Kodak 35 mm films will be encoded. These films, of course, are compatible for use in current 35 mm cameras and will not change their operation.

John Menihan, Jr.

The very high ISO 1000 speed of KODACOLOR VR 1000 Film makes it the first-choice, KODAK color-negative film for photography with a handheld camera in low light, and for stopping subject motion when you want color prints. This photograph was made at 1/125 second and f/4.

KODACOLOR VR 1000 Film

At ISO 1000, this is the highest-speed Kodak color negative film and is the film of choice for handheld photography in very dim light and for stopping action when you want color prints. The very high speed of KODACOLOR VR 1000 Film is an advantage when you want to use the highest possible shutter speed and/or gain depth of field under demanding lighting conditions. This film is capable of producing attractive results under many different light sources without camera filters due to the film's special sensitization which tends to reduce the photographic differences among a variety of light sources. The film is balanced for optimum compatibility with daylight. The film's high speed is beneficial when you want to use corrective camera filtration to achieve optimum color rendition for critical use with light sources other than daylight.

KODACOLOR VR 1000 Film has very fine grain and medium sharpness; graininess is unobtrusive in moderate-size enlargements. The film features T-GRAIN Emulsion from Kodak, a new advance in emulsion technology that provides both higher speed and finer grain. The film's exposure latitude provides pleasing results even when moderate exposure errors are made, or when the camera exposure meter system does not properly handle atypically illuminated scenes. VR 1000 film is for use in 35 mm cameras.

Some autofocus and rangefinder non-SLR 35 mm cameras have film speed dials that go up to only ISO (ASA) 400 or 800. Because of the latitude of VR 1000 film for overexposure, you can use the film in these cameras and get good results using the highest film speed setting on the dial up to 1000.

Caroline Grimes

KODACOLOR VR 400 Film

This high-speed film has an ISO speed of 400, which makes it an excellent choice as an all-around existing-light color-negative film for color prints. It can handle lighting conditions ranging from dim existing light to bright sunlight with equal ease. It is daylight-balanced, but can produce pleasing color rendition with most existing-light sources without corrective filtration over the camera lens because of the film's special sensitization characteristics, which tend to reduce the effect of illuminant differences. For more critical color balance, corrective filtration is advisable with light sources other than daylight.

This film has finer grain than KODACOLOR VR 1000 Film; the VR 400 Film has extremely fine grain and medium sharpness which produce good quality in average-size enlargements. Since a speed of ISO 400 is adequate for many existing-light subjects, this is an excellent film to use when you want fine grain and don't need the very-high film speed of VR 1000 Film.

The VR 400 Film also has wide exposure latitude to produce pleasing pictures with moderate exposure errors or when the scene lighting is difficult for the in-camera exposure meter to measure correctly. This film is available in 135, 120, and 110 sizes.

KODACOLOR VR 200 Film

This daylight-balanced ISO 200 color negative film is fast enough for handheld photography in moderately bright existing light. It is primarily compatible with daylight, but also produces good results with other light sources without camera filters when critical color rendition is not required. When necessary, you can use corrective color filtration to achieve precisely controlled color rendition with various artificial light sources. KODACOLOR VR 200 Film has high sharpness and

KODACOLOR VR 400 Film is fast enough at ISO 400 for handheld photography in relatively dim light, yet not so fast as to be inconvenient to use in bright outdoor sunlight. This is an excellent film to use when you want to photograph subjects in both existing light and outdoors in sunlight on the same roll of film. It produces good results under a wide range of light sources. Here it was exposed for 1/60 second at f/4 under fluorescent and daylight illumination and produced attractive color rendition with no corrective filtration over the camera lens.

Norm Kerr

You can take photographs with a handheld camera in moderately bright existing light when using ISO 200 KODACOLOR VR 200 Film. This film has high sharpness and shows very little graininess. This photograph was made on KODACOLOR VR 200 Film, 1/125 second at f/3.5.

displays extremely fine grain, making it an excellent choice when you wish to produce large, high-quality prints. This film is for 35 mm, 110, 126, and roll film cameras.

In addition, KODACOLOR VR Disc Film is a similar film with very high sharpness and a speed of ISO 200 for use in disc cameras.

Bruce Nett

Under relatively bright existing-light conditions you can take existing-light pictures on KODACOLOR VR Disc Film with disc cameras that have f/2.8 or faster lenses. A strip of tape was used to cover the flash to take the picture solely by the existing lighting—daylight indoors.

Tom Beelmann

With speed of ISO 100, KODACOLOR VR 100 Film is best suited to use in bright existing light or with a tripod-mounted camera. Pictures made on KODACOLOR VR 100 Film can be enlarged greatly because of the film's very high sharpness and extremely fine grain. The picture above was made on KODACOLOR VR 100 Film, 1/15 second, f/5.6.

KODACOLOR VR 100 Film

With a film speed of ISO 100, KODACOLOR VR 100 Film is best suited to bright existing-light conditions when stopping action is not a prime requirement. This film features very high sharpness, and extremely fine grain, which allows you to make greatly enlarged prints of very high quality. It is the sharpest color negative film ever made by Kodak for general consumer use.

This daylight-balanced film can yield attractive color rendition with artificial light sources without camera filters, although corrective filtration may be necessary when you need critical color rendition. If you use corrective filtration, it will usually necessitate using a tripod and relatively long exposure times to compensate for the loss of effective film speed.

KODACOLOR VR 100 Film also offers wide exposure latitude to accommodate moderate exposure mistakes. This film is sold in 135 and 120 sizes.

KODAK COLOR SLIDE FILMS

Also called color reversal, transparency, or positive films, color slide materials, such as KODACHROME and KODAK EKTACHROME Films, produce full-color slides for projection or viewing on an illuminator. The film exposed in the camera becomes the final picture, or slide, after processing. You can have color prints made directly from your color slides or via a special intermediate color negative made from a slide, called an internegative. You can also have black-and-white prints made from a black-and-white or color internegative. And you can have duplicate color slides made directly from color slides or from an internegative.

Some color-slide films are balanced for daylight and others are balanced for tungsten light sources. Gross mismatches of film and light source result in telltale color casts. Minor mismatches also result in color casts, but frequently are well within the range of viewer acceptance. This is particularly true in the context of existing-light photography, as low light levels make it difficult to perceive color nuances when on the scene and human color memory is fallible at best. Slides projected in a darkened room gain further

KODAK EKTACHROME 160 Film (Tungsten), no filter

KODAK EKTACHROME 200 Film (Daylight), no filter

Daylight Illumination

Tungsten-balanced color slide films exposed in daylight without corrective filtration produce pictures with a pronounced blue cast. Daylight-balanced color slide films exposed to tungsten light

immunity with regard to minor color discrepancies because of the absence of known-color cues in the viewing environment. In addition, as previously mentioned, the natural appearance of the existing lighting in the scene compensates to some extent for color rendition that's less than ideal because of a moderate color cast. For closely controlled color rendition, you can match both daylight and tungsten color films to many different light sources with appropriate color filters used over the camera lens providing you can accept some loss in film speed from absorption of light by the filters.

KODAK EKTACHROME 200 Film (Daylight), no filter

KODAK EKTACHROME 160 Film (Tungsten), no filter

Tungsten Illumination

without correction yield pictures with a strong yellow-orange cast. For reasonably accurate color rendition, choose a color slide film with color balance that matches the light source as closely as possible.

As a group, color slide films have relatively narrow exposure latitude, with greater tolerance for mild underexposure rather than overexposure. It's usually better to have slightly more saturation with deep rich colors from slight underexposure rather than less saturation with washed-out colors from slight overexposure. With color slide film, control of the lightness or darkness of the final picture lies directly with the photographer through exposure, because no printing step is involved. Therefore, it is especially important to expose color slide film properly.

49

When the conditions require maximum film speed, you can expose KODAK EKTACHROME Films at 1 stop or more higher film speed with push processing. Push processing is achieved by extending the time in the first developer. See page 62. A 1-stop push, which doubles the effective film speed, generally has no perceptible adverse effect on color rendition in existing-light situations. A slight increase in contrast and graininess occurs, but not to an objectionable degree. KODACHROME Films are not recommended for push processing and exposure to higher speed ratings because they are not designed for it.

KODAK EKTACHROME P800/1600 Professional Film (Daylight)

This is the speed champ of Kodak color slide films. It offers you the option of more than one very-high speed, EI 800 or 1600, depending on how much you have the film push-processed. This film is specifically designed for push processing to attain its very high speeds. If needed, you can even have the film push processed to EI 3200 or processed normally to EI 400, with some loss of quality. The film has such high speed when push-processed that you can photograph most subjects, including those in dim existing lighting, using a handheld camera with a fast lens. And when you want color slides of existing-light action with a moderate telephoto lens, this film is the prime choice.

EKTACHROME P800/1600 Film has high sharpness and satisfactory graininess characteristics. It's balanced for daylight and similar light sources, for example, carbon-arc spotlights. You can also use the film outdoors at night, but the slides will be warmer in color than those made on tungsten film. Slides taken on this film in tungsten light will have a yellow-orange cast. This is acceptable to some viewers, but if you want more natural colors, you should use the appropriate camera filters. With these filters, however, you pay a penalty because they reduce the film speed by one quarter. See the Conversion Filters table on page 60.

You obtain best image quality at speeds of EI 800 and 1600 with this film. It produces better color balance and maximum black tones than are possible with push-processed EKTACHROME 400 Film (Daylight). As with most push processing though, you lose some quality as

the speed is increased to higher values. A speed of EI 3200 permits you to take some pictures that otherwise may be impossible, but may not meet your requirements for quality. At this speed there is increased contrast and graininess, and the maximum possible black tone is less dense. Therefore, you should expose a test roll at a speed of 3200 to determine if the slides are acceptable for your needs. Also, when using the film at the lower speed of EI 400, there is a shift in color quality resulting in an overall bluish cast. Therefore, a KODAK Color Compensating Filter CC10Y is recommended for use over the camera lens for exposing at this speed.

Before you take pictures with this film, decide on the speed you want to use—800 or 1600. Then expose the whole roll at the speed you have selected and ask your photofinisher to have the film processed for that speed. The film magazine includes a write-on area where you can indicate the speed the film should be processed for. Before you expose any rolls at EI 3200, check with your photofinisher or custom processing lab to see if they offer processing for the film at this speed. More on push processing is given on page 63.

As with other Kodak professional color films, this film requires refrigerated storage at 55°F (13°C) or lower before exposure.

KODAK EKTACHROME P800/1600 Professional Film (Daylight) is an excellent choice for photography with a handheld camera and action photography in dim existing light when you require maximum speed in a color slide film. Because this film is manufactured specifically for push processing, it provides significantly better results than are possible from push-processing other EKTACHROME Films. Here the film was exposed and push-processed (Push 2) to EI 1600 so a fast shutter speed could be used. 1/125 second at f/2.8.

Bruce Nett

Gary Whelpley

Caroline Grimes

The high ISO (ASA) 400 speed of daylight-balanced KODAK EKTACHROME 400 Film (Daylight) adapts it well to existing-light photography when you want color slides. The film's richly saturated colors with full tonal values as well as fine grain and high sharpness make this a superb film for capturing low-light subjects. This photograph was exposed for 1/30 second at f/2.

A material with good definition characteristics balanced for daylight and similar light sources, KODAK EKTACHROME 200 Film (Daylight) is fast enough for use in moderately bright existing light. Its medium speed of ISO (ASA) 200 combined with high sharpness and very fine graininess make this film an excellent choice for existing-light photography when the lighting conditions are adequate. Here the photographer exposed EKTACHROME 200 Film for 1/60 second at f/5.6.

KODAK EKTACHROME 160 Film (Tungsten) has an ISO (ASA) speed of 160 and is balanced for 3200 K tungsten illumination. However, it also produces excellent color rendition with ordinary, general-purpose tungsten lamps as well as outdoors at night. This picture was taken at 1/60 second, f/2.

KODAK EKTACHROME 400 Film (Daylight)

With a film speed of ISO (ASA) 400, this film is an excellent choice for existing-light color slide photography with daylight-quality illumination, as well as with light sources that approximate daylight, such as carbon-arc spotlights. You can also use this film for outdoor night photography with results somewhat warmer in color balance than with tungsten film. It provides good action-stopping potential and permits handheld photography in all but the lowest light levels. In addition to having high speed, KODAK EKTACHROME 400 Film yields sharp, fine-grain slides. It may be filtered for compatibility with tungsten and other light sources, but the resulting loss of effective film speed may preclude handheld photography. You can also expose the film in tungsten light without camera filters so you can use a handheld camera if you don't mind yellow-orange color rendition in your slides. Some people find such slides acceptable because tungsten light appears somewhat yellowish.

You can push-process KODAK EKTACHROME 400 Film successfully to 1 or 2 stops higher speed, when necessary, to ISO (ASA) 800 or 1600. Excellent results are obtained with push processing this film to ISO (ASA) 800. There is some loss of image quality with push processing but the benefits of higher film speed are usually more important, depending on the photographic conditions. There is greater loss in quality at ISO (ASA) 1600. See the discussion on page 62.

KODAK EKTACHROME 200 Film (Daylight)

A daylight-balanced color slide film, KODAK EKTACHROME 200 Film (Daylight) has a medium speed of ISO (ASA) 200 combined with high sharpness and very fine graininess. This combination of speed and high-quality definition makes this film an excellent choice for existing-light photography with daylight and similar light sources. The film performs well for existing-light shots outdoors at night, too, producing pictures with a slightly warm color balance that many people prefer. This 200-speed film is fast enough for using a handheld camera in moderately bright existing light, depending on the speed and focal length of your camera lens.

Filtration for use with tungsten illumination is possible, but loss of effective film speed may make handheld photography with camera filters impractical. As with EKTACHROME 400 Film (Daylight), you can use the 200-speed film in your camera for handheld photography in tungsten light without filters if you can accept a yellow-orange color cast in your pictures.

You can stretch the film's utility by push-processing for a 1- or 2-stop speed increase, if necessary. When you need higher film speed though, it's better to use EKTACHROME 400 Film with normal processing for higher quality.

KODAK EKTACHROME 160 Film (Tungsten)

Balanced for use with 3200 K tungsten lights, KODAK EKTACHROME 160 Film (Tungsten) produces attractive color rendition outdoors at night and indoors with ordinary household lamps. Sharpness and graininess, which are similar to EKTACHROME 200 Film (Daylight), are excellent. EKTACHROME 160 Film (Tungsten) has an ISO (ASA) 160 speed. When you need still more film speed, you can increase the speed 1 or 2 stops by push-processing the film. Contrast and graininess are increased slightly with 1-stop push processing, but overall quality is quite good. Quality loss with 2-stop push processing of EKTACHROME Films is greater.

For scenes outdoors at night, EKTACHROME 160 Film produces slides that may appear more natural in color rendition than slides made on daylight film, especially when the lighting is predominantly tungsten. The color balance of slides taken of outdoor night subjects in existing light on the tungsten film are cooler, or more bluish, than those taken on daylight film.

You can use this film for existing daylight indoors or outdoors in the daytime for general photography with a No. 85B filter. This attribute makes EKTACHROME 160 Film (Tungsten) a good choice when you need a single all-around color-slide film for both indoor pictures and outdoor pictures at night and in the daytime.

51

Caroline Grimes

You can use daylight-balanced KODAK EKTACHROME 100 Film (Daylight), ISO (ASA) 100, for existing-light photography with a tripod-mounted camera. It features very high sharpness and very fine grain that you can exploit in brighter light levels, too, while handholding your camera. KODACHROME 64 Film (Daylight) is also daylight-balanced and rated at ISO (ASA) 64, and is even sharper and finer grained. The picture at left was made on KODAK EKTACHROME 100 Film, 1/2 second at f/16 with the camera on a tripod.

Caroline Grimes

At ISO (ASA) 40, KODACHROME 40 Film 5070 (Type A) is balanced for 3400 K photolamps but is also good for ordinary tungsten lamps. This film is best suited to photographing stationary subjects with a tripod-mounted camera. It can produce exceptionally sharp slides, and is a remarkably fine-grained film.

KODAK EKTACHROME 100 Film (Daylight) and KODACHROME 64 Film (Daylight)

You can use these 100 and 64 speed, daylight-balanced color-slide films successfully in very bright existing light in handheld cameras. You can also use them in lower light levels when it's possible and practical to mount your camera on a tripod or brace it steadily. Both films have superb definition characteristics for recording fine detail to yield slides of high quality. KODAK EKTACHROME 100 Film, ISO (ASA) 100, exhibits very high sharpness and very fine grain. KODACHROME 64 Film, ISO (ASA) 64, is even sharper and finer grained; it has extremely high sharpness and extremely fine grain, although the difference may not be immediately apparent in normal use.

However, these films are not fast enough for handheld photography in most existing lighting; you'll need a camera support for taking most pictures. You can push-process EKTACHROME 100 Film 1 or 2 stops, but it's more practical to use higher speed film. Push processing is not recommended for KODACHROME 64 Film.

You can get good results outdoors at night with these films when you use a camera support. Color rendition is on the warm side as with other daylight-balanced slide films. Using camera filters with these films for tungsten existing light is possible but usually impractical. The resulting reduction in effective film speed may require unacceptably long exposure times which can cause exposure and color balance problems. See page 61.

KODACHROME 40 Film 5070 (Type A)

This film, balanced for 3400 K photolamps, is noted for extremely high sharpness and extremely fine grain. It also produces attractive color rendition with ordinary tungsten lamps. At ISO (ASA) 40, its speed is too low for handheld photography in all but the brightest existing-light situations, but it is an outstanding choice for making extraordinarily sharp slides of stationary subjects with a tripod-mounted camera in tungsten light or outdoors at night. You can also use it in daylight outdoors with a No. 85 filter at an effective ISO (ASA) speed of 25.

KODACHROME 25 Film (Daylight)

KODACHROME 25 Film (Daylight) is the sharpest and finest-grain color-slide film that Kodak makes for general use. However, because of its low speed of ISO (ASA) 25, the film is limited almost entirely to use in a tripod-mounted camera for existing-light photography.

This daylight-balanced film is similar to KODACHROME 64 Film but has slightly better definition characteristics. The sharpness and graininess of both films are so good, though, it's not easy to see the difference between them. The use of KODACHROME 25 Film in existing light is quite similar to that of the 64-speed film except that the 25-speed film is even more limited by its low speed. It's too slow for using camera filters in existing tungsten light. In general, it's usually better in existing-light photography to use films that feature higher speed.

MATCHING COLOR FILMS TO ILLUMINATION

To obtain maximum color fidelity, scene illumination must match the light-source standard for which the film is balanced. Practically, this means selecting a film that matches the existing-light source in the scene. Even more practically, it means selecting a film that only *approximately* matches the existing-light source, since the latter seldom conforms precisely to the standard sources for which most color films are balanced. The closer the match, the more accurate the color rendition will be. You can balance image-forming light very precisely to film requirements when necessary through the use of color filters over the camera lens. Commercial photographic illustrators routinely employ filters to achieve exactly the color effects desired.

In existing-light photography, however, which places a premium on preserving the mood of the moment, literal color rendition is generally less sought after than evocative color rendition. For example, in a photograph of people gathered about a campfire, very warm, ruddy skin tones will be accepted as natural for the circumstances, even though complexions appear far more orange than usual.

COLOR TEMPERATURES OF TYPICAL LIGHT SOURCES

Open shade	Approximately 12,000–18,000 K	Sunrise–sunset	3000—3100 K
Overcast sky	Approximately 7000 K	Photolamp	3400 K
Daylight— sunlight and skylight combined	5500 K	Tungsten photographic lamps	3200 K
Electronic flash	5500—6000 K	200-watt light bulb	2980 K
Carbon arcs	5000—5500 K	100-watt light bulb	2900 K
1 hour after sunrise, 1 hour before sunset	3500—3700 K	75-watt light bulb	2820 K
		Candlelight	1800 K

In fact, fully corrected, conventional skin rendition in such a photograph would probably look unnatural and weaken the picture.

It's fortunate that total color correction is not always necessary to make compelling existing-light photographs, because the low light levels associated with existing-light photography discourage the use of the heavy filtration that may be required to achieve literal color rendition. The following discussions of various light sources and how to balance them to commonly used types of color films reflect this reality.

Many existing-light pictures actually benefit by not being corrected to exact color rendition. The picture on the top, made on tungsten-balanced KODAK EKTACHROME 160 Film (Tungsten), conveys the feeling of the candlelight scene strongly because of the very warm rendition. The picture on the bottom, made on the same film with a No. 80A filter to achieve nearly correct color balance, is much more accurate in its portrayal, but is less effective in evoking the mood of the moment. It is, in effect, too accurate to be true.

Color Temperature

When color films are described in terms of their suitability for use in daylight or tungsten light, you know instantly the broad ranges of light sources with which they are compatible. Nonetheless, you also know from everyday observation that the actual color quality of daylight varies enormously with time of day, weather conditions, and geographic location, to cite only a few variables. And tungsten light includes such diverse sources as household bulbs, photolamps, auto headlights, and Christmas tree lights. In fact, by convention, photographic daylight and tungsten light have specific values with regard to color balance.

Daylight films produce conventionally correct color rendition when exposed under illumination with a color temperature of 5500 K. Tungsten films produce conventionally correct color rendition when exposed to illumination with a color temperature of either 3200 K or 3400 K, depending on the film. Kodak films designated as tungsten are balanced for 3200 K; Type A film is balanced for 3400 K. When film and light source match, color rendition is correct.

Color temperature is a standard means of describing the color of light by comparing it to the color of a reference object heated to various temperatures. Color temperature is expressed in Kelvin using degrees as the units of measure on a temperature scale used primarily in physics. Degree increments on the Kelvin scale represent the same temperature changes as degree increments on the Celsius scale. However, the Kelvin 0 point represents −273.16°C.

Pragmatically, the key point to remember is that the higher the color temperature of a light source, the more blue-white it is. The lower the color temperature, the more red it looks. If you have ever seen an iron billet heated in a hot flame, you have witnessed a demonstration of changing color temperature. As the temperature rises, the billet changes slowly from deep red to white hot.

The great range of color temperatures spanned by these common light sources explains why a single film cannot provide correct color rendition under all conceivable shooting conditions without occasional assistance in the form of corrective filtration. And the variety of light sources encountered in everyday life clearly precludes designing a color film balanced precisely for each and every one. In practice, select the type of color film that most nearly matches the light sources you expect to encounter, then for critical color rendition use filters if you must to achieve the degree of color correctness you feel necessary. Since it is seldom practical or desirable in existing-light photography to achieve full correction all the time, console yourself, if you need consolation, with the knowledge that most viewers are unlikely to notice color imbalances of up to approximately 200 K, for example, for typical tungsten light sources used for existing lighting and for photography. Furthermore, viewers are generally willing to accept considerably greater imbalances as long as they find them attractive and/or plausible in terms of subject and setting.

Minor imbalances are often unnoticed in existing-light photographs, especially when you view each photo separately rather than directly comparing pictures with different color balance.

DAYLIGHT ILLUMINATION

Daylight, including window light and illumination from skylights, carbon arcs, electronic flash, and moonlight, match daylight-balanced color films most suitably. Color variations associated with dawn or dusk or cool north light are usually best left uncorrected, as they establish the mood and feeling of time and place. You can correct tungsten color-slide films balanced for 3200 K for use in daylight with a No. 85B amber conversion filter. This filter absorbs approximately 2/3 stop of light, in effect reducing the speed of the film by that amount. To correct Type A color slide films balanced for 3400 K for use in daylight, expose with a No. 85 amber conversion filter over the camera lens, which also absorbs 2/3 stop of light. For example, you should expose KODAK EKTACHROME 160 Film (Tungsten), which has an ISO (ASA) speed of 160 with no filter under 3200 K lights, at a film speed of 100 when filtered for compatibility with daylight. See page 60 for exposure with filters.

Converting tungsten-balanced color slide films for use in daylight is more practical than filtering daylight films to match tungsten lighting because the daylight conversion filters for tungsten films absorb less light than the tungsten conversion filters for daylight films. Here a daylight scene is rendered well on KODAK EKTACHROME 160 Film (Tungsten) exposed through a No. 85B conversion filter with only a 2/3-stop loss in film speed.

Photographs on unfiltered EKTACHROME 160 Film (Tungsten) balanced for 3200 K (top) yield slightly warm color balance when exposed with ordinary household tungsten light bulbs. More accurate, less warm rendition is obtained exposing the film through a No. 82B light balancing filter (bottom). For most existing-light applications, the unfiltered version is perfectly satisfactory. When color balance is critical, however, the more fully corrected version is preferable, despite the 2/3-stop loss in film speed with the filter.

TUNGSTEN ILLUMINATION

Tungsten lighting provided by typical household incandescent bulbs is actually warmer, more orange, than the 3200 K and 3400 K lights to which tungsten and Type A color slide films, respectively, are balanced. Nonetheless, the slightly warmer rendition this slight imbalance creates is generally attractive and desirable in existing-light photography. If you need more accurate rendition, a No. 82B light balancing filter, which absorbs 2/3 stop of light, will correct 2900 K tungsten household illumination to 3200 K balance for EKTACHROME 160 Film (Tungsten). A No. 82C light balancing filter accomplishes a similar color correction to 3400 K for KODACHROME 40 Film 5070 (Type A), and requires the same 2/3-stop exposure adjustment. Both filters are bluish.

Correcting daylight films for use in tungsten light is possible but frequently not practical in existing light because of the large amount of light absorbed by the necessary conversion filters. The

In the pictures above, exposing daylight-balanced KODAK EKTACHROME 400 Film (Daylight) in household tungsten illumination with no filter (top) produced too warm a rendition for some viewers. Using a No. 80C conversion filter significantly reduced the excess warmth (center) and only caused a 1-stop loss of film speed. Full correction with a No. 80A conversion filter (bottom) resulted in a 2-stop film-speed reduction. This would be too much color correction for some observers, considering the warm appearance of the tungsten lighting in the actual scene.

No. 80A blue filter that converts 3200 K light to daylight quality for daylight film requires a 2-stop exposure increase. The No. 80B blue filter that converts 3400 K light to daylight quality requires a 1 2/3-stop exposure increase. Using these filters would lower the effective film speed of EKTACHROME 400 Film (Daylight) to ISO (ASA) 100 and 125, respectively, from the usual ISO (ASA) speed of 400 in daylight. This wastes most of the film's sensitivity to light. In contrast, using the appropriately balanced EKTACHROME 160 Film (Tungsten) with no filter in the same situations would allow making full use of the film's ISO (ASA) 160 speed.

When the pronounced orange cast of uncorrected daylight color film in tungsten lighting is too much for subject or circumstances but full correction would mean too much loss of film speed, try partial correction with a No. 80C blue conversion filter. This filter absorbs only about 1 stop of light and yields a moderately warm rendition that many viewers find acceptable and pleasing. In existing-light situations it provides a useful compromise between the desire for correction and the need to retain as much film speed as possible. Partial correction may be preferable to a neutral, more fully corrected rendition with a darker filter, such as a No. 80A filter, that results in a larger loss in film speed.

Using One Film for Daylight and Tungsten Light Sources

If for reasons of convenience or economy you wish to standardize on a single color slide film for indoor and outdoor use, an artificial-light film with sufficient speed, such as KODAK EKTACHROME 160 Film (Tungsten), is a logical choice. Unfiltered under tungsten lighting it offers adequate speed for handheld photography in many existing-light situations both indoors and outdoors at night. You can also use this film for subjects indoors in existing daylight and outdoors in daylight with a No. 85B filter. The film still has enough speed for all-around use in average or bright daylight outdoors, providing action-stopping shutter speeds and adequate depth of field. EKTACHROME 160 Film (Tungsten) is a good film to choose when you want to take color slides in tungsten existing light and outdoors in the daytime on the same roll of film.

When you want to take color slides in fluorescent lighting, filters are usually required to produce reasonably good, natural colors. Without corrective filtration, daylight-balanced films generally produce better results than tungsten films. If you can use prints rather than slides, you're better off using color negative film, which can be filtered effectively during printing. As these fluorescent-light photographs show, unfiltered EKTACHROME 200 Film (Daylight) (top) is somewhat yellow-green. The same film produces reasonably natural rendition when exposed through CC40C + CC40M filters (center).

Unfiltered KODACOLOR VR 400 Film (above) produces good color quality through printing corrections alone, or you can use filters at the time of exposure if you need even greater color fidelity.

FLUORESCENT ILLUMINATION

Fluorescent lights are good for photography in some respects but cause problems when you want to take pictures in color. Since fluorescent lights are commonly installed in large numbers in ceiling fixtures indoors in public places and in work places, these lights provide relatively bright, even interior lighting. Fluorescent light is fine for black-and-white photographs, generally creating, soft, unobtrusive shadows, but the lighting direction from overhead is not very flattering for photographing people. Usually, the light level is high enough for handheld photography with fast films in both black-and-white and color, depending on your camera's capabilities.

Fluorescent illumination does cause color rendition problems in color photographs. Because fluorescent lamps are deficient in or completely lack certain wavelengths and have an excess of other wavelengths of the visible spectrum, these lights cannot be corrected as fully as other light sources with smooth continuous spectra. Generally, daylight color films produce more acceptable results in fluorescent illumination than tungsten films when no camera filtration is used, although some degree of yellow-green cast is normally evident, depending on the kind of fluorescent lamps in use. Tungsten film used without camera filters usually has a pronounced blue cast.

The table on the next page indicates appropriate color filtration to use with various Kodak films exposed under different types of fluorescent lighting when the need for relatively accurate color rendition outweighs the light loss and inconvenience of strong filtration. For critical color control, make exposure tests to determine if further fine-tuning of the filter pack is necessary. If you cannot determine the specific type of fluorescent tubes illuminating the scene, use the "unknown" filter recommendations in the table, which provide generally acceptable color rendition for noncritical applications.

The additional opportunities to correct color rendition in printing make color negative films such as KODACOLOR VR 1000 and KODACOLOR VR 400 Films prime choices for use in fluorescent lighting when you want color prints rather than color slides. Also, these films tolerance for light-source color variation

FILTERS FOR FLUORESCENT LIGHT   KODAK Color Film

Fluorescent Lamp	KODACOLOR VR 1000*, VR 400* VR 200, VR 100	EKTACHROME 200 and 100 (Daylight) KODACHROME 25 (Daylight)	EKTACHROME P800/1600 Professional (Daylight)‡ EKTACHROME 400 (Daylight) KODACHROME 64 (Daylight)	EKTACHROME 160 (Tungsten)	KODACHROME 40 5070 (Type A)
Daylight	40M + 40Y + 1 stop		50M + 50Y + 1⅓ stops	No. 85B + 40M + 30Y + 1⅔ stops	No. 85 + 40R + 1⅓ stops
White	20C + 30M + 1 stop		40M + ⅔ stop	60M + 50Y + 1⅔ stops	40M + 30Y + 1 stop
Warm White	40C + 40M + 1⅓ stops		20C + 40M + 1 stop	50M + 40Y + 1 stop	30M + 20Y + 1 stop
Warm White Deluxe	60C + 30M + 2 stops		60C + 30M + 2 stops	10M + 10Y + ⅔ stop	No filter None
Cool White	30M + ⅔ stop		40M + 10Y + 1 stop	60R + 1⅓ stops	50M + 50Y + 1⅓ stops
Cool White Deluxe	20C + 10M + ⅔ stop		20C + 10M + ⅔ stop	20M + 40Y + ⅔ stop	10M + 30Y + ⅔ stop
Unknown Fluorescent†	10C + 20M + ⅔ stop		30M + ⅔ stop	50M + 50Y + 1⅓ stops	40M + 40Y + 1 stop

Note: Except for the No. 85 and No. 85B filters, the filters suggested for fluorescent illumination are KODAK Color Compensating Filters (CC). Increase exposure by the amount shown in the table.

*For critcal use.

†These filters are for emergency use only, when it's not possible to determine the type of fluoresecnt lamp in use. Color rendition in pictures taken with these filters will be less than optimum.

‡Tentative data at press time.

usually produces acceptable results in fluorescent light. Regardless of whether you are using color slide, color negative, or black-and-white film, use shutter speeds longer than 1/60 second when photographing by fluorescent light to avoid uneven exposure within the frame and underexposure. This is necessary because fluorescent lights do not emit light steadily, but actually flicker rapidly in time with pulses of alternating current. This flicker is not apparent to the eye but is to the camera.

HIGH-INTENSITY DISCHARGE LAMPS

Typical high-intensity discharge lamps include Lucalox, Multi-Vapor, deluxe white mercury, clear mercury, and sodium-vapor lamps. They are often found in sports stadiums and arenas, in commercial and industrial environments, and are employed to light streets, highways, and parking lots. The filtration required to attain a semblance of good color rendition with these light sources is indicated in the accompanying table, although in

some instances it entails such a loss of light as to preclude practical application in handheld existing-light photography.

The filter table for high-intensity discharge lamps is helpful if you can find out the type of lamps in use. Considering the lighting applications of these lamps, though, in most cases it's difficult and impractical to find out what specific kinds are in use. So in most situations you're going to have to make an educated guess.

FILTERS FOR HIGH-INTENSITY DISCHARGE LAMPS   KODAK Color Film

High-Intensity Discharge Lamp	KODACOLOR VR 1000, VR 400 VR 200, VR 100	EKTACHROME 200 and 100 (Daylight) KODACHROME 25 (Daylight)	EKTACHROME P800/1600 Professional (Daylight)† EKTACHROME 400 (Daylight) KODACHROME 64 (Daylight)	EKTACHROME 160 (Tungsten)	KODACHROME 40 5070 (Type A)
General Electric LUCALOX	70B + 50C + 3 stops		80B + 20C + 2⅓ stops	50M + 20C + 1 stop	55M + 50C + 2 stops
General Electric MULTI-VAPOR	30M + 10Y + 1 stop		40M + 20Y + 1 stop	60R + 20Y + 1⅔ stops	50R + 10Y + 1⅓ stops
Deluxe White Mercury	40M + 20Y + 1 stop		60M + 30Y + 1⅓ stops	70R + 10Y + 1⅔ stops	50R + 10Y + 1⅓ stops
Clear Mercury	80R + 1⅔ stops		70R* + 1⅓ stops	90R + 40Y + 2 stops	90R + 40Y + 2 stops

Note: The filters in the table are KODAK Color Compensating Filters (CC). Increase exposure by the amount shown in the table.
Sodium vapor lamps are not recommended for critical use.

*For EKTACHROME 400 Film (Daylight) and EKTACHROME P800/1600 Professional Film (Daylight)†, use CC25M + CC40Y filters and increase exposure 1 stop.

†Tentative data at press time.

Mercury-vapor lamps on ski slope,
KODACHROME 64 Film (Daylight),
no filter.

John Vaeth

Bruce Nett

Sodium-vapor lamps, EKTACHROME 200
Film (Daylight) (top), no filter, natural
appearance of scene with yellowish cast.
EKTACHROME 160 Film (Tungsten),
(bottom), no filter, a more neutral
rendition than the daylight film version.

Kevin Twombly

Multi-Vapor lamps, EKTACHROME 200
Film (Daylight), no filter.

Fortunately, for noncritical photohobbyist needs, we can categorize these lamps into three general types that you can identify by their appearance and where they're used.

Mercury-vapor lamps are generally used for outdoor lighting for highways, streets, and parking lots. This type of lighting may also be used for small, nonprofessional playing fields for sports. These lamps usually have a slight bluish-green appearance. For noncritical purposes without resorting to camera filters, you should use daylight films. Color slides will be somewhat blue-green but should be acceptable renditions of the existing lighting. Since KODACOLOR Films for color prints allow more tolerance of color variations among light sources, they are easier to use than color slide films. The use of color negative films for prints is discussed at the end of this section.

These three views show the lighting produced by the three general types of high-intensity discharge lamps—mercury-vapor, sodium-vapor, and Multi-Vapor lamps. Mercury-vapor and sodium-vapor lamps emit light of such odd color quality that even optimum filtration may not achieve natural rendition in pictures for critical use. Multi-Vapor lamps emit light that's more like daylight in color quality and that's better for photography than the other two types of lamps. An additional complication when photographing with these light sources is the difficulty in finding out the kinds of lamps in use. For noncritical needs, daylight color-slide film without camera filters for mercury-vapor and Multi-Vapor lamps and tungsten or Type A color-slide films without camera filters for sodium-vapor lamps generally produce acceptable results. KODACOLOR Films without corrective camera filters also give acceptable color prints for noncritical purposes with all three light sources.

Sodium-vapor lamps are usually used for the same outdoor night lighting as mercury-vapor lamps. But it's easy to distinguish between the two kinds because sodium-vapor lamps have a distinctive yellowish-amber appearance. These lamps are not recommended for critical photo needs, so camera filter recommendations are not given. However, you can obtain acceptable results for less critical applications by using tungsten or Type A films for color slides without using camera filters. If you use daylight color films, color rendition in pictures will be yellowish and less than ideal but is usually tolerable for existing-light photographs because that's the way the light sources and scene appear. Of course, you can always take pictures with black-and-white film to avoid color rendition problems.

Multi-Vapor lamps are often used in sports stadiums and indoor sports arenas. These lamps emit light of good color quality for photography with daylight color slide films for noncritical uses without camera filters. Multi-Vapor lamps have been installed to illuminate many sports activities because of the recognized need for lighting suitable for color telecasts and photography. You can recognize this lighting by its use for illuminating large night sports events and its more neutral-white appearance compared with the slightly blue-green appearance of mercury-vapor lighting.

All three types of high-intensity lamps are used for indoor commercial and industrial lighting. In these locations you may be able to contact the maintenance personnel to ask them what kind of lamps are in use. Generally, color rendition is somewhat more critical in existing-light photographs taken indoors than in those taken outdoors at night.

In some older facilities or in smaller interior areas, you may find ordinary tungsten incandescent lamps in use that require tungsten or Type A color slide films for good color rendition. These tungsten lamps are the same as or similar to those used in home lighting. They are not as bright and have a slight yellowish appearance compared with mercury-vapor and Multi-Vapor lamps, and a more neutral appearance compared with sodium-vapor lamps.

When you want color prints of scenes you intend to photograph that are illuminated by high-intensity discharge lamps, the task is made easier for you because you can use color negative film. Good choices for this purpose are KODACOLOR VR 1000 and VR 400 Films which have special sensitization that tends to reduce the photographic differences among a variety of light sources. In addition, you benefit from color corrections that can be made in printing with color-negative film. However, the printing procedure may not be able to correct the color rendition entirely.

When you use high shutter speeds with high-intensity discharge lamps, such as for stop-action sports pictures, you may get streaks or underexposure effects. This is caused by the interaction of the camera shutter with the pulsing of the lamps from the 60-cycle electrical current which is so rapid it's not noticeable to the eye. These effects are most noticeable at shutter speeds higher than 1/125 second, but are unpredictable. The effect depends on many factors involved with the lighting installation. Your pictures may or may not be spoiled by it. There is less of a problem with sports stadiums or arenas that have a large number of lamps providing even illumination for the sports event.

MIXED LIGHT SOURCES

Existing-light locales are sometimes illuminated simultaneously by several light sources of different and incompatible color quality. For example, a person might be illuminated on one side by daylight streaming through a window and on the other by tungsten light from household lamps or fluorescent light from ceiling fixtures. This creates a dilemma in that balancing the film to one light source unbalances it with respect to another. There are several ways to cope. The easiest way, if you want color prints,

is to use a color negative film and balance the color as best you can in the darkroom for the most pleasing photograph. If you use color slide film, choose one of the following approaches below to fit the situation.

Outdoors at night many scenes, especially street scenes, have a multitude of different color light sources. These situations are handled differently from indoor scenes with mixed lighting and are discussed on page 59 under "Potpourri Lighting."

When a subject is illuminated simultaneously by both daylight and tungsten light, one solution is to take the picture on daylight film without a filter. In the photo top left, EKTACHROME 200 Film (Daylight) rendered daylighted areas well, but tungsten-lighted areas look too warm. Many people find this result acceptable, though, because that's the way the scene appeared. In addition, the tungsten light filled in the shadow side of the subject. Switching to EKTACHROME 160 Film (Tungsten) yielded good color in tungsten-lighted areas but daylighted areas look too blue (bottom left photo). Most people find this unacceptable—too blue. With a color imbalance, it's usually better to have a warm balance rather than cold.

If you find the first photo unacceptable (top left) and/or want more accurate color rendition, you can eliminate or minimize one light source, then choose a film in balance with the remaining illumination. On the top right, turning off the room lights and working solely by window light secured pleasing color rendition with EKTACHROME 200 Film (Daylight). The shadow side of the subject, though, is now darker because the room lights are off and aren't providing any fill light. You could either change the camera angle to photograph the subject more from the window side to minimize shadow areas or use a reflector to fill in the shadows. See page 72. Good color rendition in the last photo resulted from closing the drapes, moving the subject deeper into the tungsten-lighted room, and using EKTACHROME 160 Film (Tungsten). This, of course, has altered the composition of the original window-light scene.

When the subject is a person and the choice is between a warm color balance made on EKTACHROME 200 Film (Daylight) (top), and a cold one made on EKTACHROME 160 Film (Tungsten) (bottom), most people prefer the warm picture. The lighting for this scene was a mixture of fluorescent and tungsten light.

Eliminate Unwanted Illumination

A simple way to deal with multiple light sources of different color quality, when circumstances permit, is to eliminate the ones you don't want. In the hypothetical window-light situation cited on the preceding page, you could turn off the artificial lights and make the picture on daylight film or you might close the curtains and move the person away from the window to a part of the room illuminated primarily by tungsten sources and take the picture on tungsten film.

Choose the Dominant Source

If one light source is noticeably stronger or more widespread than another, choose film and/or filtration to favor the dominant source. Then when composing the picture, try insofar as possible to exclude from the picture, areas illuminated by secondary light sources.

Mixed Lighting of Equal Proportions

Sometimes the different light sources are equally strong and affect roughly equal areas of the scene. If you balance to daylight, tungsten-lighted subject matter will be rendered very warm, or yellow-orange. If you balance to tungsten, daylighted subject matter will be rendered very cool, or coldly blue. Decide which option will let you make a picture that looks the way you want it to look and proceed accordingly. When skin tone is involved, the warmer rendition will usually be preferable.

The Skin-Tone Factor

Although preferences in color balance are very much a matter of personal taste, most viewers agree broadly about one thing: Where skin-tone rendition is concerned and color rendition is less than ideal, warm yellow-orangish rendition is better and more pleasing than cold rendition. Whenever people are prominent in the picture, avoid excessively cold, bluish rendition because it makes people look cadaverous. If you cannot achieve perfect color balance, err on the side of warmth and you'll nearly always be safe.

Potpourri Lighting

Some existing-light subjects contain so many different light sources of such varied color quality that the concept of "correct color balance" is totally inapplicable. A carnival midway or a cityscape at night, for example, can easily boast an array of lights ranging in color quality from daylight through candlelight, from blue-white to cherry red. Your guiding principle here is that daylight film will render the scene more warmly and tungsten film will render it more coldly. Neither choice is inherently better except in terms of making the picture look the way you want it to look. If you prefer a yellow-orange, or a warm rendition, daylight film is better. If you prefer a more blue, or cold, rendition, tungsten film is better.

Scenes containing a jumble of light sources of widely differing color quality should be photographed on whatever film type will produce a color rendition you like. A daylight-balanced film, such as EKTACHROME 400 Film (Daylight) (top), yields a warmer rendition than a tungsten-balanced film, such as EKTACHROME 160 Film (Tungsten) (bottom). KODACOLOR Film—color-negative film—will let you choose a rendition you like through filtration when printing. For outdoor night pictures color rendition is usually not critical and is a matter of personal choice.

59

USING FILTERS

The colored filters commonly used to balance image-forming light to match film type, adjust color for effect, or fine-tune it subtly all share one basic characteristic: They absorb light. Filters work their magic not by adding their own color to the light reaching the film but rather by subtracting light of complementary color. Color filters always prevent some light from entering the camera. Consequently, whenever you use colored filters, you have to increase exposure enough to compensate for the light the filter does not let reach the film. The accompanying tables indicate the exposure corrections required for conversion, light balancing, and Kodak color compensating filters. These filters are sold by photo dealers.

As low light levels normally encountered in existing-light photography leave little leeway for further loss of light, heavy filtration should be avoided when possible. When you foresee a need for strong filtration, choose the fastest suitable film and consider pushing the film speed, too, if possible. This helps attain reasonable exposure settings that will permit a shutter speed adequate for handholding your camera or that will yield adequate action-stopping and depth of field for the circumstances.

Many through-the-lens exposure meter systems can compensate accurately for colored filters' light absorption. Some cannot. And many non-SLR cameras have meter cells that do not read through lens attachments. If your camera exposure meter cannot correct automatically for filter use, meter the exposure with no

Color compensating filters are normally used to effect relatively small changes in color rendition. Light balancing filters effect moderate shifts in color balance and are most often used to correct light of nonstandard color temperature to either 3200 K or 3400 K. Conversion filters induce substantial changes in color temperature needed to match standard artificial light sources to daylight films or to match daylight to films balanced for artificial light. You can also use all of these filter types to create imaginative, offbeat color effects. Kodak manufactures these filters in economical gelatin filter squares in 2-inch (50 mm), 3-inch (75 mm), 4-inch (100 mm), and 5-inch (125 mm) sizes, as well as some larger sizes.

CONVERSION FILTERS

To Convert	Use Filter Number	Filter Color	Exposure Increase in Stops*
3200 K to Daylight 5500 K	80A	Blue	2
3400 K to Daylight 5500 K	80B	Blue	1 2/3
3800 K† to Daylight 5500 K	80C	Blue	1
4200 K‡ to Daylight 5500 K	80D	Blue	1/3
Daylight 5500 K to 3800 K	85C	Amber	1/3
Daylight 5500 K to 3400 K	85	Amber	2/3
Daylight 5500 K to 3200 K	85B	Amber	2/3

*For critical work, check these values by practical test.
†Aluminum-filled clear flashbulbs, such as 25 and 26.
‡Zirconium-filled clear flashbulbs, such as AG-1 and M3.

LIGHT BALANCING FILTERS

To Obtain 3200 K from:	To Obtain 3400 K from:	Use Filter Number	Filter Color	Exposure Increase in Stops*
2490 K	2610 K	82C + 82C		1 1/3
2570 K	2700 K	82C + 82B		1 1/3
2650 K	2780 K	82C + 82A		1
2720 K	2870 K	82C + 82	Bluish	1
2800 K	2950 K	82C		2/3
2900 K	3060 K	82B		2/3
3000 K	3180 K	82A		1/3
3100 K	3290 K	82		1/3
3200 K	3400 K	No Filter Necessary	—	—
3300 K	3510 K	81		1/3
3400 K	3630 K	81A		1/3
3500 K	3740 K	81B	Yellowish	1/3
3600 K	3850 K	81C		1/3
3700 K	3970 K	81D		2/3
3850 K	4140 K	81EF		2/3

*These values are approximate. For critical work, you should check them by practical test, especially if you use more than one filter.

KODAK COLOR COMPENSATING FILTERS

Peak Density	Yellow (Absorbs Blue)	Exposure Increase in Stops*	Magenta (Absorbs Green)	Exposure Increase in Stops*	Cyan (Absorbs Red)	Exposure Increase in Stops*
.025	CC025Y	—	CC025M	—	CC025C	—
.05	CC05Y	—	CC05M	1/3	CC05C	1/3
.075	CC075Y	—	CC075M	1/3	CC075C	1/3
.10	CC10Y	—	CC10M	1/3	CC10C	1/3
.20	CC20Y	1/3	CC20M	1/3	CC20C	1/3
.30	CC30Y	1/3	CC30M	2/3	CC30C	2/3
.40	CC40Y	1/3	CC40M	2/3	CC40C	2/3
.50	CC50Y	2/3	CC50M	2/3	CC50C	1

Peak Density	Red (Absorbs Blue and Green)	Exposure Increase in Stops*	Green (Absorbs Blue and Red)	Exposure Increase in Stops*	Blue (Absorbs Red and Green)	Exposure Increase in Stops*
.025	CC025R	—	CC025G	—	CC025B	—
.05	CC05R	1/3	CC05G	1/3	CC05B	1/3
.075	CC075R	1/3	CC075G	1/3	CC075B	1/3
.10	CC10R	1/3	CC10G	1/3	CC10B	1/3
.20	CC20R	1/3	CC20G	1/3	CC20B	2/3
.30	CC30R	2/3	CC30G	2/3	CC30B	2/3
.40	CC40R	2/3	CC40G	2/3	CC40B	1
.50	CC50R	1	CC50G	1	CC50B	1 1/3

*These values are approximate. For critical work, you should check them by practical test, especially if you use more than one filter.

filter first with your camera's film speed dial set for the speed of the film without a filter, adjust the exposure setting *manually* to compensate for the filter, then install the filter and take the picture. It's easier to do than to contemplate. A different method for doing this is given on page 69.

To determine whether your exposure meter works correctly through color filters, compare the camera exposure settings made through the filter with the exposure settings of the same scene obtained without, but adjusted for, the filter. Use the film speed recommended for without a filter in both situations. If the camera settings are the same, the meter reading through that particular filter is reliable. Note that in this case when the through-the-lens meter reading compensates correctly for the light absorbed by the filter, you set the speed of the film without a filter on the film-speed dial of your camera or meter.

RECIPROCITY EFFECTS AND COMPENSATION FOR COLOR FILMS

In photography, the law of reciprocity states that brief exposure to much light should produce the same effect on film as proportionately longer exposure time to less light. For example, all other factors being constant, an exposure of 1/8 second at $f/1.4$ should theoretically affect film the same as a 16-second exposure at $f/16$. In fact, the law of reciprocity does not hold true at extremely short or long exposure times. With color films, failure of the law of reciprocity at longer-than-normal exposure times manifests itself as underexposure and otherwise inexplicable deviations from normal color rendition since each color layer in the film's emulsion may have different reciprocity effects. In existing-light photography the reciprocity effects of extremely short exposure times are not of interest.

The accompanying table provides reciprocity data for a variety of Kodak color films, indicating how much additional exposure to give at different long exposure times and what correction filters, if any, to use to restore more normal color balance. In practice, the nonstandard color quality inherent in many existing-light scenes tends to mask small to moderate deviations in exposure and color rendition. As a rule, it is better to avoid reciprocity effects than to have to correct

EXPOSURE AND FILTER COMPENSATION FOR RECIPROCITY CHARACTERISTICS   KODAK Color Films

KODAK Film	Exposure Time in Seconds						
	1/10,000	1/1000	1/100	1/10	1	10	100
KODACOLOR VR 1000	None No Filter				+1 stop CC10G	+2 stops CC20G	+3 stops CC30G+CC10B
KODACOLOR VR 400	None No Filter				+1/2 stop No Filter	+1 stop No Filter	+2 stops No Filter
KODACOLOR VR 200	None No Filter				+1 stop CC10R	+2 stops CC10R+CC10Y	Not Recommended*
KODACOLOR VR 100	None No Filter				+1 stop CC10R	+2 stops CC10R+CC10Y	Not Recommended*
EKTACHROME P800/1600 Professional (Daylight)†	None No Filter				Not Recommended*		
EKTACHROME 400 (Daylight)	None No Filter				+1/2 stop No Filter	+1 1/2 stops CC10C	+2 1/2 stops CC10C
EKTACHROME 200 (Daylight)	None No Filter				+1/2 stop No Filter	Not Recommended*	
EKTACHROME 160† (Tungsten)	None CC025G	None CC05C	None No Filter		+1/2 stop CC025M	Not Recommended*	
EKTACHROME 100 (Daylight)	None No Filter				Not Recommended*		
KODACHROME 64 (Daylight)	None No Filter				+1 stop CC10R	Not Recommended*	
KODACHROME 25 (Daylight)	None No Filter				+1/2 stop No Filter	Not Recommended*	
KODACHROME 40 5070 (Type A)	None No Filter				+1/2 stop No Filter	5 Seconds: +1 stop No Filter	10 and 100 Seconds: Not Recommended*

Note: The exposure increase, in lens stops, includes the adjustment required by any filter(s) suggested.
*Not recommended for critical use.
†Tentative data at press time.

them. Unless there are compelling reasons to do otherwise, use film fast enough to let you work at shutter speeds short enough to avoid the problem altogether.

PROCESSING *KODAK* COLOR FILMS

For best results, you should have color films processed promptly after they are exposed. Kodak Processing Labs provide color processing services for Kodak color negative and color slide films in 135 size, disc, 110 and 126 cartridges, and popular roll sizes. Additional services include making color prints and enlargements from color negatives, color slides, and color prints; color slides from color negatives or from color slides; and color negatives from color slides and color prints. These services are available through photo dealers or in many cases directly from Eastman Kodak Company via convenient, prepaid KODAK Processing Mailers sold by photo retailers.

Other photofinishers and color processing laboratories also offer these services. See your photo dealer.

You can process KODAK EKTACHROME and KODACOLOR Films yourself in KODAK Film Processing Kits that are sold through photo dealers. Process EKTACHROME 100, 160, 200, 400, and P800/1600 Films in the KODAK EKTACHROME Film Processing Kit, Process E-6, or KODAK HOBBY-PAC™ Color Slide Kit. Process KODACOLOR Films in the KODAK FLEXICOLOR® Processing Kit, Process C-41, or in the KODAK HOBBY-PAC™ Color Negative Film Kit. One exception is KODACOLOR VR Disc Film which is not recommended for processing in the home darkroom. Kodak materials for making your own color prints from color negatives or color slides are also available in quantities suitable for the home darkroom and are designed for this use. Detailed instructions are included with Kodak processing kits.

You can't process KODACHROME Films successfully in your own darkroom because the process is highly complex and requires commercial photofinishing equipment.

Costas

Push-processing KODAK EKTACHROME Films allows you to double or quadruple the film speed to stop movement better with higher shutter speeds, or obtain greater depth of field by using smaller lens openings in existing light. This picture was photographed on EKTACHROME 160 Film (Tungsten) rated at ISO (ASA) 320 and push-processed 1 stop. Allegro Brillante,' starring Peter Martins, courtesy New York City Ballet.

Push-Processing KODAK EKTACHROME Films

As noted earlier, when you need more film speed than the standard speed rating provides, you can obtain good results with KODAK EKTACHROME Films by doubling the ISO (ASA) speed and push-processing the film by extending the development time. The accompanying table shows how much to increase time in the first developer when push processing KODAK EKTACHROME Films in KODAK EKTACHROME Film Chemicals, Process E-6, or the KODAK HOBBY-PAC™ Color Slide Kit to double the film speed and also, for emergency use, to quadruple the standard speed. Changes in graininess and contrast that occur when doubling film speed are unlikely to be noticed in most existing-light applications. Increased graininess and contrast resulting from pushing to four times the normal ISO (ASA) speed are more noticeable, but are unlikely to be objectionable for noncritical purposes for low-light subjects.

Note that from the standpoint of obtaining optimum picture quality it is preferable to expose a high-speed film at its normal speed or the speed it's designed for than to push a film with less speed to a higher-than-normal speed. And remember that push processing affects an entire roll of film. You cannot push-process just part of a roll because it's impractical to separate exposures requiring extended development from those needing only normal processing. To avoid mix-ups that could spoil pictures, prominently mark containers holding exposed film that requires push processing with the notice: PUSH TO 800 (or applicable speed number). If possible, keep these containers separate from film that you want to have processed normally. Be sure to reset the film speed dial on your camera or handheld exposure meter to the normal speed value when you've finished exposing a roll at a boosted film speed. It will help reduce the likelihood of inadvertently underexposing a following roll should you forget to check the film speed setting on the meter.

KODAK EKTACHROME P800/1600 Professional Film (Daylight) is intended for push processing to one stop for a speed of EI 800 or to two stops for a speed of EI 1600. Under adverse conditions you can push-process the film to EI 3200, but with a loss in quality. You obtain better quality at the 800 and 1600 speeds. Film speeds of 400, 800, 1600, and 3200 are printed on the film magazine which has a writeable surface. Circle the amount of push processing you want. Circle "400, E-6" when you want normal processing for EI 400, which is a secondary use for this film that requires a yellow camera filter. See page 50.

KODACOLOR and KODACHROME Films are not recommended for push processing because they are not designed for it. Push processing with these films can cause color casts in highlights and shadows along with increased contrast and graininess. In addition, with KODACOLOR Films the color rendition problems cannot be fully corrected in printing. And since KODACOLOR Films are negative films, there is no significant speed increase, based on shadow detail, obtained with push processing.

PUSH-PROCESSING *KODAK EKTACHROME* FILMS

ISO (ASA) Film Speed					*KODAK EKTACHROME* FILM CHEMICALS, PROCESS E-6		*KODAK HOBBY-PAC™* COLOR SLIDE KIT
EKTACHROME P800/1600 Professional (Daylight)	EKTACHROME 400 (Daylight)	EKTACHROME 200 (Daylight)	EKTACHROME 160 (Tungsten)	EKTACHROME 100 (Daylight)	Change the time in the first developer by	Or change the temperature of the first developer by	Change the time in the first developer at 100°F (38°C) by
EI 800	800	400	320	200	+2 minutes	+8°F (+4.4°C)	+4 minutes
EI 1600	1600	800	640	400	+5 minutes	+12°F (+6.7°C)	+6 1/2 minutes
EI 3200*	—	—	—	—	+10 minutes	+16°F (+8.9°C)	+9 1/2 minutes†

Push processing results in some loss in quality compared with normal exposure and processing, but can enable you to obtain photographs under otherwise unsuitable conditions.

Refer to the chemcial instructions for more complete information.

*Because of loss of quality at this high film speed, test the procedure before using.

†For push processing to EI 3200, the color developer must be diluted and the time increased to 14 minutes in this solution.

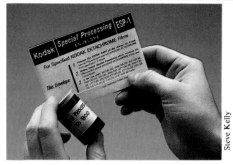

Steve Kelly

One-stop push-processing to double the film speeds of KODAK EKTACHROME P800/1600, EKTACHROME 400, EKTACHROME 200, and EKTACHROME 160 Films, and EKTACHROME 100 Film when necessary, is available from Kodak Processing Labs and other laboratories. Purchase a KODAK Special Processing Envelope, ESP-1, from your photo dealer for each roll you want to have push-processed by Kodak.

KODAK Special Processing

Kodak Processing Labs provide push processing of KODAK EKTACHROME P800/1600, EKTACHROME 400, EKTACHROME 200 (Daylight), and EKTACHROME 160 (Tungsten) Films and when necessary, EKTACHROME 100 Film (Daylight) to double their standard film speed ratings. The service is offered for films in 35 mm and 120-size rolls.

To obtain 1 stop push processing by Kodak, purchase a KODAK Special Processing Envelope, ESP-1. (This process is also referred to as "Push 1".) You can then give the envelope containing the film to your photo dealer for Kodak processing, or send it directly to a U.S. Kodak Processing Lab in an appropriate prepaid Kodak mailer. The price of the KODAK Special Processing Envelope, ESP-1, is in addition to the standard processing charge.

You can have KODAK EKTACHROME P800/1600 Professional Film (Daylight) push processed by Kodak when you use the KODAK ESP-1 Envelope, described

Don Buck

The film magazine for KODAK EKTACHROME P800/1600 Professional Film (Daylight) has a writeable surface so that you can indicate the speed for which the film should be processed. Circle the speed you used to expose the film.

Bruce Nett

above, for processing the film to EI 800, Push 1: Circle "800 P1" on the film magazine. When you want P800/1600 film processed to a film speed of EI 1600, Push 2, request it from your photo dealer but do not use the ESP-1 Envelope for processing to the 1600 speed: Circle "1600 P2" on the film magazine. If you want the film processed to EI 400, circle "400, E-6" on the film magazine and have the film processed normally without push processing. Do not use the ESP-1 Envelope. Push 3 processing for P800/1600 film to EI 3200 is not available from Kodak.

Kodak Processing Labs offer Push 2 processing for KODAK EKTACHROME P800/1600 Professional Film which is specifically designed for extended push-processing techniques.

Other photofinishers and other color processing laboratories also offer push processing for KODAK EKTACHROME Films. Ask your photo dealer about their service.

KODAK BLACK-AND-WHITE FILMS FOR EXISTING LIGHT

Although human eyes perceive a world of color, some of the most compelling photographs ever made have been made in black-and-white. For the existing-light photographer, high-speed black-and-white films, such as KODAK TRI-X Pan Film, facilitate working in low light of uncertain color quality. Most of the Kodak black-and-white films suitable for existing-light photography with a hand-held camera are inherently fast films. The broad exposure latitude of many popular black-and-white films allows capturing contrasty and/or unevenly lighted scenes that virtually defy optimum rendition on narrow-latitude color-slide materials.

KODAK TRI-X Pan Film, at ISO (ASA) 400, offers the existing-light photographer high film speed, excellent image quality, and complete freedom from concerns about color balance. Some of the most dramatic and expressive existing-light photographs have been made in black-and-white.

Black-and-white films generally have more latitude for overexposure than for underexposure. Excessive overexposure will lead to loss of definition and increased graininess.

For all practical purposes, you can ignore concerns about the color quality of ambient light. And if you need an even higher film speed number than the film provides with normal processing, you can easily push-process most high-speed black-and-white films so you can expose at twice the normal ISO (ASA) speed with minimum loss of quality simply by extending development time. From an aesthetic standpoint, working in black-and-white offers unparalleled opportunity to control the image through coordinated adjustments in exposure, processing, and printing.

KODAK TRI-X Pan Film

For all-around existing-light photography, KODAK TRI-X Pan Film, ISO (ASA) 400, offers the combination of high speed, fine graininess, and very high sharpness, plus great exposure latitude, and a "look" that makes it the primary black-and-white film of many photographers, regardless of light level. For many years, because of its excellent quality and versatility, it has been the film of choice for photojournalists and sports photographers who must capture moving subjects in light ranging from desert glare to coal-bin murk.

Bruce Nett

Linda C. Economan, KINSA

In reasonable light levels, KODAK PLUS-X Pan and VERICHROME Pan Films, ISO (ASA) 125, can produce pictures with high sharpness and little perceptible graininess, even when greatly enlarged. This photograph was made on PLUS-X Pan Film.

KODAK PLUS-X Pan and VERICHROME Pan Films

In bright existing light, KODAK PLUS-X Pan and VERICHROME Pan Films, ISO (ASA) 125, combine adequate speed with extremely fine graininess and sharpness great enough to permit making exquisitely detailed enlargements of considerable size. Both films have excellent exposure latitude so they're forgiving when exposure is less than optimum.

The speed kings among Kodak black-and-white films for very low light are KODAK Recording Film 2475, film speed 1000, in 135 size, and KODAK ROYAL-X Pan Film, film speed ISO (ASA) 1250, in 120 size. Although coarser-grained than slower films, they significantly extend the lower light-level limits of photography with a handheld camera. This photograph was made at 1/250 second and f/4 on Recording Film 2475.

KODAK Recording Film 2475 and KODAK ROYAL-X Pan Film

Somewhat more specialized in application because of their more pronounced graininess are the Kodak black-and-white speed kings, KODAK Recording Film 2475, speed 1000, available in 135-size 36-exposure magazines, and KODAK ROYAL-X Pan Film, ISO (ASA) 1250, available in 120-size rolls. When necessary, you can expose these films at even higher speed numbers by push-processing the film. See page 65.

KODAK PANATOMIC-X Film and KODAK Technical Pan Film 2415

Two lower speed Kodak films of interest for use in existing-light photography are KODAK PANATOMIC-X Film, ISO (ASA) 32, and KODAK Technical Pan Film 2415, film speed 25. These films have the best definition characteristics of any Kodak black-and-white films for general use. PANATOMIC-X Film offers extremely fine graininess and very high sharpness and is recommended for use with standard developers. Tech Pan film features even finer grain and extremely high sharpness for the ultimate in pictorial black-and-white image quality for Kodak films. The film's amazing definition specifications provide excellent enlargements at magnifications of 25X and even 50X. Tech Pan film requires a special developer, like KODAK TECHNIDOL LC Developer, sold by photo dealers, for pictorial purposes.

Tom Beelmann

KODAK Technical Pan Film 2415 is an incredible film for capturing detail—it has the highest resolution and finest grain of any pictorial black-and-white film Kodak has ever made! You can now make sharp enlargements of excellent quality up to 50X or larger depending on your camera lens. Because of the film's speed of 25, use it for bright existing-light subjects or put your camera on a tripod. Exposed at 1/30 second at f/4.7.

You could use one of these lower speed films when you want the best definition for large prints with high degrees of enlargement. To use these films in a handheld camera, the subject should be in very bright existing light, such as window light, or your camera should be mounted on a tripod for taking pictures in existing light of average brightness. For existing-light photography, these films are more adaptable to photographing inanimate, stationary subjects where the use of slow shutter speeds presents no problems with subject motion.

Tom Beelmann

ISO (ASA) 400, 1/30 second, normal processsing

Film speed number 800, 1/60 second, push-processed with 50 percent increase in development time

Film speed number 1600, 1/125 second, push-processed with 50 percent increase in development time

PROCESSING *KODAK* BLACK-AND-WHITE FILMS

There are several ways you can have your black-and-white film processed. If you have your own equipped darkroom, you're all set to be creative and enjoy processing and printing black-and-white film. If you're not experiencing the fun of doing your own darkroom work yet, you can have your black-and-white film processed by Kodak which offers this service for KODAK TRI-X Pan, VERICHROME Pan, PLUS-X Pan, and PANATOMIC-X Films. To obtain Kodak processing, take your film to a photo dealer who offers Kodak processing services. You can also have your film processed by other photo-finishers or custom processing labs.

Push-Processing Black-and-White Films

When the light is too low to permit convenient photography at the ISO (ASA) speed rating of the black-and-white film in your camera, you can underexpose the film by 1 to 2 stops, then increase development time to push-process the film. As a suggested starting point, try increasing the normal recommended development time by 50 percent. You may find later that you prefer to print from negatives that have been developed somewhat less or perhaps a trifle more, but the 50-percent increase will put you safely in the ball park.

Push-processing black-and-white films is most successful when photographing in soft, even lighting that does not exaggerate subject contrast. Under such conditions, a 1- or even 2-stop push can produce acceptable results. With moderately

Push-processing black-and-white films works best when scene contrast is low or average. These photographs were made on TRI-X Pan Film at speed ratings of 400, 800, 1600, and again at 800. In the first three pictures made at the same lens opening (above), scene contrast was average and all three pictures are acceptable, although understandably different. The photo taken at the normal speed of the film, ISO (ASA) 400, displays the best image quality, while the push-processed shots show progressively more loss in quality, especially shadow detail, as the film is exposed at higher film speed numbers. For the last picture (bottom right), scene contrast was increased through harsh lighting, and a 1-stop push produced a marginally acceptable print with little detail visible outside of medium- and bright-tone areas.

Tom Beelmann

Film speed number 800, push-processed with 50 percent increase in development time

contrasty subjects, consider a 1-stop push the maximum boost likely to permit making a fairly normal-looking print with good quality. Since extended development cannot put shadow detail on film that the film has not recorded, the less shadow detail in the scene the better. In contrasty situations, set exposures to render middle tones and highlights appropriately, and try to compose your pictures so that large shadow areas are excluded or are used dramatically to reinforce the mood. It is an irony of black-and-white photography in existing light that the scenes that are most likely to impel you to push film speed tend to be harsh and contrasty, with many under-lighted areas, while low-contrast scenes that respond well to pushing are least likely to require it. Generally, with high-

contrast scenes that have harsh lighting, which produces brilliant highlights and deep black shadows, you should expose the film at its normal ISO (ASA) speed and process the film normally without push processing.

Black-and-white negative film that has been underexposed a moderate amount, such as 1 stop, and push-processed with a 50-percent increase in development time should produce negatives that are more printable and prints of better quality than *underexposed* film processed normally. Prints from push-processed negatives should have acceptably good quality but will show less shadow detail, increased contrast, and increased graininess. This slight loss in quality is usually acceptable when you consider the increased benefits of more versatile camera

EXPOSURE AND DEVELOPMENT COMPENSATION FOR RECIPROCITY CHARACTERISTICS   KODAK Black-and-White Films

KODAK Film	Exposure Time in Seconds	$\frac{1}{100,000}$	$\frac{1}{10,000}$	$\frac{1}{1000}$	$\frac{1}{100}$	$\frac{1}{10}$	1	10	100
TRI-X Pan PLUS-X Pan* VERICHROME Pan PANATOMIC-X*	Increase Lens Opening by	+1 stop	+½ stop	None	None	None	+1 stop	+2 stops	+3 stops
	Or Use Corrected Exposure Time in Seconds	Use Lens Opening Correction	Use Lens Opening Correction	No Change	No Change	No Change	2	50	1200
	Change Developing Time by	+20 percent	+15 percent	+10 percent	None	None	−10 percent	−20 percent	−30 percent
Recording 2475	Increase Lens Opening by	—	None	None	None	None	+⅔ stop	+1⅓ stops	+2⅓ stops
	Change Developing Time by	—	None	None	None	None	−10 percent	−20 percent	−30 percent
Royal-X Pan	Increase Lens Opening by	—	—	None	None	None	+1 stop	+2 stops	+3 stops
	Or Use Corrected Exposure Time in Seconds	—	—	No Change	No Change	No Change	2	50	1200
	Change Developing Time by	—	—	+10 percent	None	None	−10 percent	−20 percent	−30 percent
Technical Pan 2415	Increase Lens Opening by	—	—	None	None	None	None	+⅔ stop	+1⅓ stops
	Or Use Corrected Exposure Time in Seconds	—	—	No Change	No Change	No Change	No Change	—	—
	Change Developing Time by	—	—	None	None	None	None	None	None

*Information also applies to KODAK PLUS-X Pan Professional and PANATOMIC-X Professional Films.

techniques possible with a 1-stop higher film speed number.

An important point to understand about push processing black-and-white negative film is that it doesn't significantly increase the speed of the film. Film speed, which is related to shadow detail, is inherent in the manufacture of negative films and cannot be increased significantly by merely extending the development time. As mentioned before, increasing the development time does not add shadow detail on the film where detail is deficient from underexposure. When shadow detail is not there to develop, push processing cannot create it and therefore does not fully compensate for underexposure, the result of exposing the film at a higher film speed number. Push processing does give better looking prints from moderately underexposed negatives than with normal processing.

When the normal speed of the film is adequate for the picture-taking situation, you'll obtain the highest image quality when you expose and process your film according to normal recommendations.

For additional information about push processing Kodak black-and-white films, consult the book *KODAK Films— Color and Black-and-White (AF-1).*

RECIPROCITY EFFECTS FOR BLACK-AND-WHITE FILMS

Black-and-white film, like color film, is subject to exposure anomalies when exposed for unusually short or long exposure times. Reciprocity effects in black-and-white include apparent loss of film speed and contrast changes. The accompanying table suggests exposure increases and adjustments in developing times to correct reciprocity effects with most general-purpose Kodak black-and-white films.

In many existing-light settings, lighting and subject contrast tend to mask minor deviations from normal rendition, so you can ignore mild reciprocity effects. If you anticipate pronounced reciprocity effects, you should consider the corrections suggested in the table as starting points for personal experimentation to determine what exposure and development modifications work best for you. If you must mix normal exposures and very long ones on the same roll of film, do not apply the development adjustments listed in the table because they will adversely affect the normally exposed frames. Instead, adjust the exposure as indicated and develop the roll normally, then you can rely on contrast control in printing to

This table suggests exposure and development adjustments for correcting reciprocity effects with KODAK general-purpose black-and-white films. If you must mix normal and long exposures on one roll of film, make the indicated exposure adjustments but develop the roll normally and control contrast as necessary when printing.

produce an image that looks like the picture in your mind's eye.

As in existing-light color photography, the best way to deal with reciprocity effects in black-and-white is to avoid them altogether by using film fast enough so you don't need to use excessively long exposure times.

KODAK FILM TABLES FOR EXISTING-LIGHT PHOTOGRAPHY

The following tables list and summarize the characteristics of a selection of Kodak color and black-and-white films suited to existing-light photography. Additional information about many of these and other Kodak films will be found in the book *KODAK Films, AF-1,* sold by photo dealers.

KODAK BLACK-AND-WHITE FILMS FOR EXISTING-LIGHT PHOTOGRAPHY

KODAK Film	Description	Film Speed	Definition			Degree of Enlargement Potential‡	Roll Sizes Available	Processed by
			Graininess	Resolving Power	Sharpness			
TRI-X Pan	A high-speed panchromatic film especially useful for photographing existing-light subjects, fast action, subjects requiring good depth of field and high shutter speeds. This film has fine grain and excellent quality for such a high speed.	ISO (ASA) 400	Fine	High	Very High	Moderate	135-20 135-36 120	Kodak, other labs, or users
PLUS-X Pan*	An excellent, general-purpose panchromatic film that offers the optimum combination of medium speed and extremely fine grain. For use in 35 mm cameras.	ISO (ASA) 125	Extremely Fine	High	Very High	High	135-20 135-36	Kodak, other labs, or users
VERICHROME Pan	An excellent, general-purpose panchromatic film that offers the optimum combination of medium speed and extremely fine grain. For use in cartridge and roll-film cameras.	ISO (ASA) 125	Extremely Fine	High	Very High	High	110-12 126-12 120, 127	Kodak, other labs, or users
Recording 2475	A very high-speed panchromatic film for use in situations where the highest film speed is essential and fine grain is not important to you, such as for taking action photographs where the light is poor. The film has extended red sensitivity and coarse grain. For use in 35 mm cameras.	EI 1000	Coarse	Medium	Very High	Low	135-36	Other labs or users
ROYAL-X Pan	A very high-speed panchromatic film for use in situations where the highest film speed is essential and fine grain is not important to you, such as for taking action photographs where the light is poor. The film has medium grain and is for use in 120-size cameras.	ISO (ASA) 1250	Medium	High	High	Moderately Low	120	Other labs or users
PANATOMIC-X*†	An extremely fine-grain panchromatic film with very high sharpness for big enlargements.	ISO (ASA) 32	Extremely Fine	Very High	Very High	Very High	135-20 135-36	Kodak, other labs, or users
Technical Pan 2415†	An extremely fine-grain panchromatic film with extremely high sharpness for giant-size enlargements. The film has extended red sensitivity and is for use in 35 mm cameras.	EI 25	Extremely Fine	Extremely High	Extremely High	Extremely High	135-36	Other labs or users

*This information also applies to the professional versions of these films in 120 size.

†These films generally require slow shutter speeds and the use of a tripod to hold your camera steady for existing-light pictures because of the films' low speeds.

‡For good-quality negatives.

KODAK COLOR FILMS FOR EXISTING-LIGHT PHOTOGRAPHY

KODAK Film	Description	Type of Picture	Type of Existing Light	ISO (ASA) Speed	Graininess	Resolving Power	Sharpness	Degree of Enlargement Potential¶	Roll Sizes Available	Processed by
KODACOLOR VR 1000	A very high-speed color negative film for color prints. Use this film for photographing existing light, fast action, and subjects requiring good depth of field and high shutter speeds. It's designed to produce pleasing results using the existing illumination without camera filters. The film has wide exposure latitude and great versatility.	Color prints	Daylight, tungsten, fluorescent, or outdoors at night	1000	Very Fine	Medium	Medium	Moderately Low	135-12 135-24 135-36	Kodak, other labs, or users Process C-41
KODACOLOR VR 400	A high-speed color negative film for color prints. Use this film for photographing existing light, fast action, and subjects requiring good depth of field and high shutter speeds. It's designed to produce pleasing results using the existing illumination without camera filters. The film features wide exposure latitude, extremely fine grain, and great versatility.	Color prints		400	Extremely Fine	Medium	Medium	Moderate	135-12 135-24 135-36 120 110-12 110-24	
KODACOLOR VR 200*	A medium-speed, general-purpose color negative film. It's also useful for existing light, fast action, and subjects requiring good depth of field or high shutter speeds. It has extremely fine grain, excellent sharpness, and good versatility.	Color prints		200	Extremely Fine	High	High	High	135-12 135-24 135-36 110-12 110-24 126-12 126-24 620 127	
KODACOLOR VR 100	A medium-speed, general-purpose color negative film which yields color prints. Features extremely fine grain, and wide exposure latitude. It's excellent for big enlargements.	Color prints		100	Extremely Fine	High	Very High	High	135-12 135-24 135-36 120	
KODACOLOR VR Disc†	A color negative film for color prints that features the excellent combination of medium speed, very high sharpness, and micro-fine grain for use in disc cameras. This is a general-purpose film with enough speed for some brightly lighted existing-light subjects, depending on the capabilities of the camera.	Color prints		200	Micro Fine	High	Very High	Very High	Disc-15	Kodak and other labs Process C-41A

KODAK Film	Description	Type of Picture	Type of Existing Light	ISO (ASA) Speed	Graininess	Resolving Power	Sharpness	Roll Sizes Available	Processed by
EKTACHROME P800/1600 Professional Film (Daylight)	A very high-speed color slide film for photographing existing light, fast action, and subjects requiring good depth of field and high shutter speeds. The film is very useful for pictures under adverse lighting conditions. To attain its high speed, the film requires push processing to EI 800 or 1600, or even higher, if necessary.	Color slides	Daylight, fluorescent, or outdoors at night	EI 800††	—	—	—	135-36	Kodak, other labs, or users Process E-6P Push
				EI 1600‡‡	Moderately** Coarse	Medium**	High**		

Film	Description	Form	Light source	Speed (ISO/ASA)	Graininess	Sharpness	Resolving Power	Sizes	Processing
EKTACHROME 400 (Daylight)	A high-speed, color slide film for existing light, fast action, and subjects requiring good depth of field and high shutter speeds. It has fine grain and good sharpness. This film can be push-processed to double the speed.	Color slides	Daylight, fluorescent, or outdoors at night	400 800††	Fine —	Medium —	High —	135-20 135-36 120	Kodak, other labs, or users Process E-6
EKTACHROME 200 (Daylight)§	A medium-speed, color slide film for existing light, fast action, and subjects requiring good depth of field or high shutter speeds. It has very fine grain and excellent sharpness. This film can be push-processed to double the speed.	Color slides	Daylight, fluorescent, or outdoors at night	200 400††	Very Fine —	High —	High —	135-20 135-36¶¶	
EKTACHROME 160 (Tungsten)	A medium-speed, color slide film for use with 3200 K tungsten lamps and existing tungsten light. It features the same very fine grain and excellent sharpness as the 200-speed Daylight Film. This film can be push-processed to double the speed.	Color slides	Tungsten or outdoors at night	160 320††	Very Fine —	High —	High —	135-20 135-36¶¶	
			Daylight with No. 85B filter	100 No. 85B§§ 200†† No. 85B§§	Very Fine —	High —	High —		
EKTACHROME 100 (Daylight)‡	A medium-speed, color slide film for general all-around use. This film produces vivid color rendition and has excellent sharpness and graininess characteristics.	Color slides	Daylight, fluorescent, or outdoors at night	100	Very Fine	High	Very High	135-20 135-36 120¶¶	
KODACHROME 64 (Daylight)	A medium-speed, general-purpose film for color slides. Exhibits remarkable sharpness and freedom from graininess. Color rendition of this film is excellent.	Color slides	Daylight, fluorescent, or outdoors at night	64	Extremely Fine	High	Extremely High	135-20 135-36 110-20 126-20¶¶	Kodak and other labs Commercial Laboratory Process K-14
KODACHROME 40 5070 (Type A)§	A color slide film designed for use with 3400 K photolamps. It also produces good results in existing tungsten light. The film gives high-quality color rendition and exceptional definition. You can also take pictures in daylight with the recommended conversion filter.	Color slides	Tungsten or outdoors at night	40	Extremely Fine	High	Extremely High	135-36	
			Daylight with No. 85 filter	25 No. 85§§					
KODACHROME 25 (Daylight)§	A popular color slide film noted for excellent color and high sharpness. It has extremely fine grain and good exposure latitude.	Color slides	Daylight, fluorescent, or outdoors at night	25	Extremely Fine	High	Extremely High	135-20 135-36¶¶	

Note: Generally for noncritical purposes, you can obtain acceptable color balance with the films recommended for fluorescent and tungsten existing light without using camera filters. For critical color rendition, however, you should use the recommended filters. See pages 54—60.

* A similar film, KODACOLOR VR Disc Film, is available for disc cameras. See table.

† To use KODAK Disc Cameras for existing-light pictures, the subject must be relatively brightly lighted for proper exposure unless your subject is within the recommended flash distance range. See the discussion on page 90.

‡ EKTACHROME 64 Film (Daylight), a similar film with an ISO (ASA) speed of 64 is available in 110-20 and 126-20 sizes. The professional version of this film is sold in 135 and 120 sizes.

§ These films generally require slow shutter speeds and the use of a tripod to hold your camera steady for existing-light pictures because of the films' low speeds.

¶ For good quality negatives.

** Tentative data at press time.

†† You can expose these films in 135 and 120 sizes at the higher speeds given here when you use the KODAK Special Processing Envelope, ESP-1 (Push 1), sold by photo dealers. See page 63.

‡‡ You can expose this film in 135 size at EI 1600 when you request Push 2 processing to EI 1600 from your photo dealer. Kodak offers this service.

§§ When using filters with in-camera exposure meters that can make incorrect meter readings through the filter, set the film speed dial on your camera for the speed of the film with the filter, make the meter reading *before* you put the filter on the camera, and adjust the camera exposure settings. Then put the filter on your camera without changing the settings and take the picture. See your camera manual.

¶¶ Professional versions of these films are available in 135 and 120 sizes. KODACHROME Professional Films are available only in 135 size. EKTACHROME 100 Professional Film (Daylight), in roll film, is only available in 120 size.

Existing-Light Pictures at Home

The home environment and existing-light photography are a natural combination. The ordinary and sometimes extraordinary events of daily life at home provide a wealth of subjects, and the direct, uncomplicated techniques of existing-light photography permit recording them easily and naturally. Today's cameras with high-speed lenses and high-speed films allow impromptu, handheld photography to be interwoven into the fabric of everyday life without disrupting the activity, and allow the existing-light photographer to remain a full participant in the events he or she is recording.

Kodak-Pathé

Norm Kerr

The following pointers on taking existing-light photographs at home will help you anticipate commonly encountered photographic situations and deal with them successfully to obtain good pictures.

INDOOR LIGHT LEVELS

If you're not accustomed to photographing indoors without flash, you may be surprised at first to note how much less bright home lighting is compared with bright outdoor lighting conditions in the daytime. Your exposure meter responds properly to the low light levels of indoor existing light, but it often appears to your eye that there's more light on the scene than there actually is. That's because the human eye has a remarkable capacity to adapt to a very wide range of lighting conditions, functioning well in bright sun or dim candlelight. In fact, the average living room with a light-colored ceiling, at night with all the lights turned on in the room, is usually illuminated to a light level approximately 1/800 that of outdoor sunlight. For example, the typical exposure for subjects in average living room lighting on KODACOLOR VR 1000 Film is 1/30 second at $f/2.8$. Using the same film outdoors to record a front-lighted scene on a sunny day would require exposure settings of 1/1000 second at $f/16$.

Effective photography indoors with a handheld camera usually requires a high-speed film and a high-speed lens to keep shutter speeds fast enough to negate camera and/or subject movement. And don't overlook the possibility of push-processing color slide or black-and-white film so you can expose it at a higher film-speed number as described in the chapter

KODACOLOR VR 1000 Film, 1/30 second $f/4$

The major and minor events of daily life at home are natural subjects for existing-light photography. You can capture them easily with modern cameras and high-speed films.

on Kodak films. This is beneficial when you're confronted with really dim environments and have difficulty getting enough exposure at the shutter speeds required for handholding your camera.

DAYLIGHT INDOORS

From dawn to dusk, many areas of the home may be lighted primarily by daylight and only secondarily, if at all, by artificial light. When daylight is dominant, use daylight-type color slide or color negative films and consider turning off or otherwise avoiding the effects of secondary light sources that differ in color quality from daylight. Whether to turn the room lights on or off in the daytime for existing-light pictures is a matter of personal choice. Turning on the room lights may help fill in harsh shadows and reduce scene contrast, and will result in a higher light level. This works well with black-and-white film as you don't have to be concerned with color balance. But with daylight color film, since household lamps are usually tungsten, the parts of your subject illuminated by these light sources will appear warm or yellow-orange while the daylight portions will appear cooler and more neutral in color rendition. Some people do not object to this lighting mismatch and find it acceptable. See the photos on page 58. If truer color rendition is important, turn off the artificial light sources and consider reducing scene contrast by using one of the following methods.

Direct Sunlight

When the sun shines directly into a room, the potential exists for high scene contrast that may exceed the latitude of the film. In small rooms with white or light walls and ceilings this is less likely to be a problem than in large rooms with less-reflective surfaces. The side of the subject facing the window will be brightly illuminated while other parts will be comparatively deeply shadowed. You can reduce the contrast several ways.

Tom Beelmann

Direct sunlight flooding a small room with white or light walls and ceiling doesn't produce too much contrast because the walls and ceiling act as reflectors, bouncing light into areas that would otherwise be deeply shadowed. In a large room with dark walls and ceiling, direct sunlight provides hard, contrasty illumination because the walls and ceiling are too dark to bounce light effectively into the shadows.

71

No reflector

With reflector

Tom Beelmann

Use an improvised reflector, in this case a projection screen, to bounce fill light into shadow areas you wish to lighten to reduce contrast. The closer the reflector the brighter the fill light, but don't place it so close to the subject that it intrudes into the picture.

Improving the Existing Lighting

Although an existing-light purist might consider it cheating, you can reduce excessive scene contrast by adding light to the shaded areas of the subject to bring them into closer relationship with the brightly lighted areas. Strictly speaking, this is not true existing light but the appearance in the photo is very similar to it. You can use reflectors to bounce light where it is needed, for example. You can improvise reflectors from projection screens, large sheets of card stock, such

as photographic mount boards, crumpled and then flattened aluminum foil, white sheets, pillow cases, or even newspaper pages that aren't too densely filled with print. The more efficient the reflector and the closer it is to the subject, the more the shadows will be filled with light. Do not use a colored reflector with color film unless you want a special effect. An exception to this advice is to use gold colored aluminum foil to add warmth to a subject illuminated by window light from a blue or overcast sky.

Use Fill-In Flash

If you have a KODAK Disc Camera, the built-in flash will automatically fire to supplement window light except in bright circumstances. With other types of cameras you can use accessory flash units to fill in shadow areas with daylight-quality light either by aiming the flash directly at the subject or by bouncing the light of the flash from a nearby reflecting surface.

The technique of using fill-in flash is to adjust the intensity of the flash so it's 1, 2, or 3 stops less than the main lighting on the subject. See the discussion about fill-light intensities in the next section. First, make an exposure meter reading of the subject area most brightly lighted by the ambient lighting as seen from the camera position. Say the exposure is 1/30 second at $f/5.6$ with KODACOLOR VR 400 Film and you want the shadows to be 2 stops darker than the highlighted areas. Always select the camera settings indicated by the meter reading which includes a shutter speed recommended for the proper flash synchronization for your camera and flash unit. Most cameras with focal-plane shutters will also synchronize at

Tom Beelmann

When window light is too contrasty to produce a pleasing picture (left), you can reduce the contrast by using a flash unit to lighten the shadows (right). Lighting the shadows with fill to 1 stop less bright than the highlights produced a natural-looking, pleasing picture on KODAK EKTACHROME 200 Film (Daylight). The fill light was from a flash unit, but a reflector could have done as well. Consult camera and flash owner's manuals for specific operating instructions for your equipment.

slower shutter speeds than the highest speed recommended for electronic flash. See your camera owner's manual.

Next, set the controls on an automatic electronic flash unit for a lens opening 2 stops *larger* than the lens opening you'll use on your camera to take the picture. In the example, since $f/5.6$ is the camera setting, you would set the auto flash for $f/2.8$. This adjusts the flash to give 2 stops less light, which underexposes the shadows by 2 stops and results in the desired amount of fill-in.

You can do this by adjusting the flash unit controls for the lens opening and flash distance range or by changing the flash power setting to 1/2 or 1/4 power if your unit has this feature. The half-power setting gives 1 stop less light and the quarter-power setting 2 stops less light than full power. Consult the owner's manual accompanying your flash unit for specific instructions about fill-flash operation. Note, that this fill-in flash technique won't work with through-the-lens autoflash exposure systems. With these systems, you should set the flash on manual for fill-in flash and follow the suggestions given below for manual units.

If your flash unit does not have any of these controls, you can change the amount of fill-in by setting the flash on manual and moving it closer to or farther away from the subject or by covering the flash reflector with layers of white handkerchief to achieve the proper amount of fill-in. One layer of handkerchief reduces the light by two stops and cuts the flash-to-subject distance in half. You can either use a zoom lens to help frame your subject in the viewfinder or use a flash extension cord, sold by photo dealers, to position the flash unit separately from the camera at the proper distance. Here again the objective is to adjust the intensity of the flash to give 2 stops less light. For the example given, adjust the flash for $f/2.8$. Since this provides sufficient light for proper exposure at a lens opening 2 stops larger than the one you're actually going to use on the camera, the flash fill-in intensity results in the desired 2-stops underexposure of the shadows. This will require some experimenting. Consult the flash exposure calculator on your flash unit.

Don't use colored bounce surfaces to provide fill light in color photography unless you deliberately wish to change the color of the filled-in area. Here, light reflected by a blue card discolors the shadow area (left). A white card reflector produces a warmer, more natural rendition (right).

Keep It Looking Natural

For natural-looking fill-in illumination, don't overdo the technique. You can obtain pleasing results with color negative films when the fill-lighted areas are illuminated about 2 to 3 stops less than the daylighted areas. This ratio also works well with most black-and-white films. With color slide films, light the shadows about 1 to 2 stops less than the daylighted areas. There is no hard-and-fast rule about precisely how much fill light to use, because the right amount is whatever makes the picture look the way you want it to look. Experience is the best guide.

When bouncing daylight, flash, or tungsten light, use white bounce surfaces if possible or light neutral-colored surfaces when shooting in color. Bouncing light from colored surfaces will impart an overall color cast to the picture. In black-and-white, the color of the bounce surface doesn't matter much except that light surfaces are more efficient reflectors than dark ones.

The contrasty picture (top) was made by direct sunlight flooding through the window. The softer version (bottom) was made after drawing the translucent curtains. Closing the curtains lowered the light level by 1 stop, but improved the picture.

Soften the Daylight

If windows in the picture-taking area are furnished with white or neutral-colored translucent curtains, close them to take the edge off harsh sunlight. Sheer or translucent curtains will diffuse the light and soften overall contrast appreciably. This is an excellent technique when photographing people.

Move the Subject and/or the Camera

Sometimes the easiest way to cope with window light when it's harsh is to change the subject's orientation to it, and/or the camera position relative to the subject and light source. For example, instead of photographing a person half-lighted by a window on your left side, move so the window is completely behind you and turn the subject appropriately. Be careful not to cast your shadow on the subject or elsewhere in the picture area.

Sometimes moving the subject deeper into the room, away from the window, will result in more-even lighting. If the window isn't too large, try moving the subject to one side where he or she is illuminated by diffused rather than direct light.

You cannot relocate a window but you can change camera and subject positions relative to it to secure more pleasing lighting effects. Here the photographer moved so that the window would light the subject frontally (left), from behind the camera position, rather than from the side (right).

Indirect Daylight

One of the most pleasing forms of existing light is soft, indirect daylight. It may be produced by sunlight reflecting from a blue sky in classic north-skylight fashion, or it may be a gentle suffusion of diffused daylight from an overcast day permeating the room. Lighting effects are much softer than those produced by direct sunlight and normally do not require any supplementary fill-in illumination. The lighting from an overcast sky is even better when there is snow on the ground to reflect additional soft lighting into the room on the first or second floor.

Indirect daylight is usually fairly cool in color quality. Color slide films exposed by this lighting often exhibit a cool, or slightly bluish, color cast. It is seldom objectionable in pictures of things, but may cause unpleasant skin-tone rendition in pictures of people. If you are photographing people on slide film, you may prefer to warm up the rendition with a No. 1A skylight filter over your camera lens. The filter is colorless and requires no additional exposure, but will remove the excess blue associated with indirect daylight. The filter is not necessary with color negative or black-and-white films.

Indirect daylight provided by sunlight reflected from the sky or from cloud cover is much softer than direct sunlight. Fill-in illumination is usually not necessary as long as the subject is not backlighted.

Determining Exposure for Indoor Daylight

Normal exposure meter techniques work well when the overall contrast is low to moderate. If the lighting is harsh and/or uneven, make close-up readings of significant subject tones. If you are using fill-in illumination, make bright- and dark-area readings as you adjust the fill light until you attain the desired relationship between light and dark tones. Be careful to exclude the window itself and other light sources from the exposure meter's field, or they will inflate the reading. If you are photographing against the light, with the subject between the camera and the window, it is particularly important to avoid reading the window inadvertently. If you do, you will greatly underexpose the subject. On the other hand, if you wish to make a silhouette, read the window area, excluding the subject from the meter field, and expose as the meter indicates.

ARTIFICIAL LIGHT INDOORS

Artificial light indoors tends to fall into one of two broad categories: tungsten light, associated with home lighting, and fluorescent illumination, common to business and commercial establishments but also used for some home lighting. As a rule, for color slides use tungsten-balanced color films for photographing by tungsten light and use daylight-balanced color films, with or without corrective

Tom Beelmann

When a window is behind the subject, don't let the exposure meter read the window unless you want to create a silhouette (top). Instead make a close-up meter reading of the subject to obtain proper exposure of the subject. However, this causes the window area to be overexposed (center). Also, shooting toward the window can cause the subject area to exhibit some possible camera flare. It's usually better to change your camera and/or subject position so the subject is lighted from the front or side by the window light (bottom). EKTACHROME 200 Film (Daylight)

filtration, for photographing in fluorescent light. You can use Kodak color negative and black-and-white films freely with tungsten and fluorescent lights.

Lighting effects produced by tungsten lamps are often quite different from those obtained with fluorescent tubes because of the different ways the two light sources are usually installed. Tungsten lighting is typically marked by pools of light near lamps, with darker areas separating them. The overall effect is often contrasty.

For taking pictures in tungsten existing lighting at home, household lamps with translucent shades are best. These shades diffuse the light, and increase the light level by transmitting a large proportion of the light from the lamp. Diffusing the light softens the shadow areas in the room and reduces contrast.

Generally it's beneficial to turn on all the lights in the room for taking existing-light pictures. This helps make the lighting brighter and less contrasty. You can also increase the home lighting level by substituting higher wattage tungsten bulbs or by turning the switch for three-way lamps to the brightest setting. This increases the light level without affecting the modeling or realism of the existing lighting. Do not use photographic lamps in household lighting fixtures or exceed the wattage rating specified for the light fixture.

Fluorescent lights are frequently installed in multitube banks or ceiling fixtures that spread light quite evenly over large areas. However, keep in mind that the overhead light sources can create unattractive shadows on people's faces resulting in near-black eye sockets or other mournful-looking effects on film.

The facial shadows cast by overhead fluorescent fixtures can be lightened with fill from reflectors. Direct flash fill is difficult to balance to fluorescent color quality, and vice versa. However, you can improve the color quality of pictures taken under fluorescent illumination by bouncing light from electronic flash off a white ceiling or by using camera filters. For pleasing informal portraits with color slide films, the best solution by far is to seek a different environment illuminated by daylight or tungsten sources.

Kodak Pathe'

Indoor tungsten lighting tends to be uneven and therefore contrasty. Typically, there are bright islands of light emerging from a darker sea.

Tom Beelmann

Multiple-tube fluorescent lighting is often quite even. Customary overhead installations cast shadows beneath objects, where they are less obvious, and the shadows are usually neither intense nor sharply defined. The top lighting though sometimes creates deep, exaggerated shadows in people's eye sockets, which look unattractive in close-up photographs (top). Fill the shadows with a reflector, or have the subject tilt his or her head slightly upward toward the light (bottom). Better yet, move to a more favorable location. EKTACHROME 200 Film (Daylight), cool white lamps, CC30M filter, no reflector fill-in.

Tom Beelmann

A lighted lamp in the background put the girl's face in shadow. Moving the camera captured more pleasing lighting on the subject. EKTACHROME 160 Film (Tungsten) with ESP-1 Processing.

Watch the Shadows

With existing light it is especially important to pay attention to the shadows. There is an inevitable law of lighting that each and every light source creates not only a highlight area but also a complementary shadow area. One consequence of this is that indoor lighting, which is normally provided by multiple light sources in a given area, can produce conflicting highlights and shadows in a single picture. In real life, these effects aren't bothersome and generally pass unnoticed. In pictures, however, they can be very disturbing and create considerable visual confusion.

View indoor subjects and settings critically and pay special attention to shadow placement as well as intensity. Frame scenes so that extraneous or confusing shadows will be outside the picture area. A table or chair casting three or four separate and distinct sets of shadows in different directions can be an unsettling and unpleasant distraction in an otherwise attractive picture. When you cannot frame the picture to avoid multiple shadows, move the subject or turn off or relocate lights to solve the problem.

When you're taking pictures of a person or a pet, observe the shadows on your subject. Generally you should avoid photographing the subject with the face all in shadow as it would be with a household lamp illuminating the subject from behind. You can avoid this by asking your subject to move to obtain more favorable lighting on the front or side of the face or possibly by moving the lamp that's behind the subject. Also, remember that turning on other lights in the room helps lighten the shadows and increases the light level.

Bruce Nett

Bounce lighting from a photolamp made the room illumination more even and increased the light level for handheld picture-taking. EKTACHROME 160 Film (Tungsten), 1/30 second, halfway between f/2.8 and f/4.

Adding Fill Light

Fill lighting, discussed in terms of complementing daylight, can also be applied in many tungsten-lighted situations. Reflectors or suitable room surfaces can bounce supplementary tungsten illumination. You can use extra household lamps bounced or aimed directly or photolamps bounced to supplement existing tungsten lighting. This means you won't be taking true existing-light pictures but this additional light can often improve the existing lighting without spoiling its natural appearance.

Adding fill light can reduce the lighting contrast and increase the light level. Bounce light from a 500-watt photolamp aimed at a white ceiling in addition to the room lighting can increase the amount of light by about 6 times. This extra illumination may let you use a shutter speed fast enough to handhold your camera or use a smaller lens opening for increased depth of field depending on the speed of the film you're using and the speed of your camera lens. Since bounce lighting makes the illumination more uniform, you can often use the same exposure for different locations around the room in the general vicinity of the bounce lamp. This is especially convenient for taking pictures during a party or for photographing active subjects.

A 500-watt reflector photolamp in a clamp-on light socket makes a versatile bounce light. Both are sold by photo dealers. You can use a 3200 K or 3400 K photolamp; however, the former is closer in color to tungsten household lamps. Place the lamp about 3 to 5 feet from the ceiling and aim the lamp toward the ceiling area between your camera and your subject. Adjust the photolamp so it doesn't illuminate the subject directly and overpower the existing lighting. *Use caution when using photolamps because they become very hot and will shatter like other light bulbs when broken.*

Use the bounce-light exposure table for planning purposes or as an exposure guide if your exposure meter isn't working.

SUGGESTED EXPOSURES FOR BOUNCE LIGHTING WITH A 500-WATT REFLECTOR-TYPE PHOTOLAMP PLUS ROOM LIGHTS

Kodak Film	ISO (ASA) Film Speed	Shutter Speed	Lens Opening
For Color Prints			
Kodacolor VR 1000	1000	1/60 sec	f/5.6
Kodacolor VR 400	400	1/60 sec	f/4
Kodacolor VR 200	200	1/30 sec	f/4
Kodacolor VR 100	100	1/30 sec	f/2.8
For Color Slides			
Ektachrome P800/1600 Professional (Daylight)	EI 800*†	1/60 sec	f/5.6
	EI 250† with No. 80B filter	1/30 sec	f/4
	EI 1600*‡	1/125 sec	f/5.6
	EI 500‡ with No. 80B filter	1/60 sec	f/4
Ektachrome 400 (Daylight)	400*	1/60 sec	f/4
	125 with No. 80B filter	1/30 sec	f/2.8
	800*†	1/60 sec	f/5.6
	250† with No. 80B filter	1/30 sec	f/4
Ektachrome 200 (Daylight)	200*	1/30 sec	f/4
	400*†	1/60 sec	f/4
	125† with No. 80B filter	1/30 sec	f/2.8
Ektachrome 160 (Tungsten)	160	1/30 sec	f/2.8 ↓ 4
	320†	1/30 sec	f/4 ↓ 5.6
Ektachrome 100 (Daylight)	100*	1/30 sec	f/2.8
Kodachrome 64 (Daylight)	64*	1/30 sec	f/2
Kodachrome 40 5070 (Type A)	40	1/15§ sec	f/2 ↓ 2.8
For Black-and-White Prints			
Tri-X Pan	400	1/60 sec	f/4
Verichrome Pan Plus-X Pan	125	1/30 sec	f/2.8

Note: The ⌐↓⌐ symbol indicates the lens opening halfway between the two f-numbers.

*Pictures taken with daylight film and no filter will look yellow-red.
†With ESP-1 Processing—sizes 135 and 120.
‡With Push 2 Processing.
§For shutter speeds slower than 1/30 second, use a firm camera support.

Determining Exposure for Artificial Light Indoors

Close-up exposure meter readings of significant subject tones or incident-light meter readings at the subject position are the safest bases for determining exposure indoors under artificial light. In tungsten-lighted areas, be sure to exclude lamps and light fixtures from a reflected-light meter's field or they will boost the reading too high for correct exposure of average-toned subject matter. In fluorescent-lighted areas, don't make exposure readings with the camera or handheld meter tilted upward to an extent that ceiling fixtures are included in the reading area. And remember to use shutter speeds slower than 1/60 second under fluorescent illumination to avoid uneven exposure or underexposure, even when the light level tempts you to choose higher shutter speeds. In general, rely on accurate meter readings or an exposure table to determine camera settings. Indoor lighting can be deceptive even for highly experienced photographers, and brightness (or darkness) levels are often other than what they seem to the human eye.

PHOTOGRAPHING TELEVISION AND COMPUTER SCREEN IMAGES

Another interesting form of existing-light photography at home is the recording of images from your television screen. The fleeting electronic pictures glowing on the screen may represent important history in the making, dramatic sports action, lighthearted entertainment, or simply scenes of beauty worth preserving for another look at another time. Or perhaps you want conventional still pictures of personal events you've captured with a

Photographing images on a television screen lets you preserve fleeting moments that may range from historic events to personal pleasures. Photographed from English television on Kodacolor Film.

James H. V. Bright

home video recorder. Whatever the reason, it's easy to do. You'll need reasonably fast daylight-balanced color film or black-and-white film and a tripod, a cable release, and a camera that can focus close enough to fill the frame with the TV image.

You can also use the techniques given in this section to photograph important information or an interesting design you've created on your home computer display screen. These computers may use your home television set as a display screen or a computer monitor that is quite similar to a conventional TV.

With the KODAK INSTAGRAPHIC CRT Print Imager, users can produce high-quality instant color photographs of static 9-, 12-, 13- or 19-inch computer sreen displays on instant KODAK INSTAGRAPHIC Color Print Film. The outfit includes a KODAK INSTAGRAPHIC Camera Back and a KODAK INSTAGRAPHIC Print Module with lens and shutter mounted on a cone. The cone helps you center and position the camera at the correct distance for framing and focus while blocking out the room lights from the surface of the image screen. Exposure is automatically determined by the camera. The INSTAGRAPHIC Camera is intended for photographing screen images that remain stationary and don't change during the exposure which may be approximately 4 seconds.

Adapter brackets, supplied with the outfit, allow you to substitute a 35 mm single-lens-reflex camera when you want conventional slides or prints, or want to photograph transitory images on television or computer screens. The KODAK INSTAGRAPHIC Imager is available from photo dealers who sell Kodak professional and audio visual products.

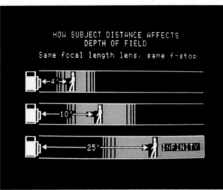

Caroline Grimes

You can also use the same techniques for photographing TV images to photograph your home computer display screen. EKTACHROME 200 Film (Daylight), 1/8 second between f/4 and f/5.6, exposure increased for dark background.

Norm Kerr

Norm Kerr

The KODAK INSTAGRAPHIC CRT Print Imager (bottom photo) gives photographers an automated means of photographing static computer screen displays. The outfit features a KODAK INSTAGRAPHIC Camera that produces instant color prints on KODAK INSTAGRAPHIC Color Print Film. The unit is designed for 9-, 12-, 13-, or 19-inch screen sizes. For obtaining conventional color prints and color slides of both television and computer screen images, you can use a 35 mm SLR camera. Adapter brackets for this purpose are provided with the outfit (top photo).

Adjust TV Picture and Computer Screen Image Quality

Begin by adjusting your TV set or computer screen to deliver a picture or image of slightly lower than normal contrast and adjust the brightness control so the image shows some detail in both highlight (light) and shadow (dark) areas. If necessary, adjust the color controls to produce visually pleasing color quality. If your TV set or computer monitor has an automatic brightness control that varies picture brightness in response to changing levels of room lighting, switch the automatic system off and control the brightness manually. This will prevent the set from changing picture brightness when you turn off the room lights.

If you can't turn the sensor off, put a piece of black tape over the sensor to prevent it from working. This dims the screen and permits you to adjust the brightness manually.

Position the Camera Carefully

Mount your camera on the tripod, level it side to side and front to back, then adjust the height until the center of the camera lens is exactly the same height above the floor as the center of the TV or computer screen. Position the tripod and camera so the lens axis is exactly perpendicular to the face of the TV screen. Fill the viewfinder of the camera with the TV or computer screen image insofar as possible. With some camera types it may be necessary to use supplementary close-up attachments to fill the frame with the TV or computer screen image. If you are not using an SLR camera, consult the owner's manual as to how to correct for parallax, the difference at close ranges between what you see through the finder and what the film "sees" through the camera lens.

When making minor adjustments in camera position for framing, raise or lower the tripod column to effect changes in vertical placement of the image and slide the tripod itself sideways to change lateral position. This procedure helps maintain parallelism between the film in the camera and the TV screen.

SUGGESTED CAMERA SETTINGS FOR PICTURES OF TELEVISION AND COMPUTER DISPLAY SCREEN IMAGES

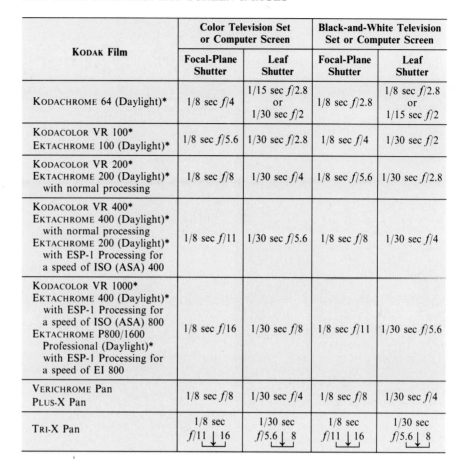

KODAK Film	Color Television Set or Computer Screen		Black-and-White Television Set or Computer Screen	
	Focal-Plane Shutter	Leaf Shutter	Focal-Plane Shutter	Leaf Shutter
KODACHROME 64 (Daylight)*	1/8 sec f/4	1/15 sec f/2.8 or 1/30 sec f/2	1/8 sec f/2.8	1/8 sec f/2.8 or 1/15 sec f/2
KODACOLOR VR 100* EKTACHROME 100 (Daylight)*	1/8 sec f/5.6	1/30 sec f/2.8	1/8 sec f/4	1/30 sec f/2
KODACOLOR VR 200* EKTACHROME 200 (Daylight)* with normal processing	1/8 sec f/8	1/30 sec f/4	1/8 sec f/5.6	1/30 sec f/2.8
KODACOLOR VR 400* EKTACHROME 400 (Daylight)* with normal processing EKTACHROME 200 (Daylight)* with ESP-1 Processing for a speed of ISO (ASA) 400	1/8 sec f/11	1/30 sec f/5.6	1/8 sec f/8	1/30 sec f/4
KODACOLOR VR 1000* EKTACHROME 400 (Daylight)* with ESP-1 Processing for a speed of ISO (ASA) 800 EKTACHROME P800/1600 Professional (Daylight)* with ESP-1 Processing for a speed of EI 800	1/8 sec f/16	1/30 sec f/8	1/8 sec f/11	1/30 sec f/5.6
VERICHROME Pan PLUS-X Pan	1/8 sec f/8	1/30 sec f/4	1/8 sec f/8	1/30 sec f/4
TRI-X Pan	1/8 sec f/11 ↓ 16	1/30 sec f/5.6 ↓ 8	1/8 sec f/11 ↓ 16	1/30 sec f/5.6 ↓ 8

Note: The ↓ symbol indicates the lens opening halfway between the two f-numbers. Use the exposures for black-and-white TV sets and computer display screens for monochrome computer screens that display the image in black-and-white or one color only, such as green.

Important: With focal-plane shutters, use a shutter speed of 1/8 second or slower. With leaf shutters, use a shutter speed of 1/30 second or slower. These precautions are necessary to prevent dark streaks in your pictures. See discussion in text. Use a tripod or other camera support for shutter speeds slower than 1/30 second.

*You can obtain acceptable color rendition in pictures of color television without the use of camera filters. For critical rendition with KODACOLOR Films, however, use a KODAK Color Compensating Filter CC10B over your camera lens. Increase the exposure suggested in the table by 1/3 stop. For critical rendition with KODACHROME and EKTACHROME Films listed in the table, use a KODAK Color Compensating Filter CC3OR and increase the suggested exposure by 1/2 stop.

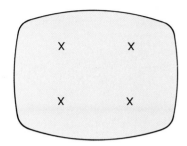

After you have properly aligned your camera with the TV or computer screen (see text), focus on a part of the TV screen about 1/2 the distance from the center toward a corner. Appropriate focus points are indicated by Xs in the illustration. This results in a reasonable compromise focus setting that allows for the curvature of the TV or computer screen. Stopping the lens down moderately then provides the necessary depth of field to cover the center and edges of the screen.

Focus for Overall Sharpness, Darken the Room

With an SLR camera, focus on the TV or computer screen at a point about 1/2 the distance from the center of the screen toward a corner. That helps achieve a good overall focus despite the curvature of the face of the picture tube. With a rangefinder camera, focus on picture detail in the center of the screen; then "cheat" the focus a hair to a slightly more distant setting on the focusing scale to achieve the same type of compromise setting.

To eliminate reflections on the face of the TV picture or computer image tube, turn off all room lights. During the day, draw the blinds to prevent daylight from washing out the TV picture or causing reflections on the tube. Do not use flash or photolamps to illuminate the image display screen because these light sources would overpower the TV or computer image and you would get a picture of a blank screen.

Determine Exposure by Meter or Table

Determine exposure by referring to the accompanying table or by making a close-up reading of the TV or computer screen image with a reflected-light exposure meter. If you haven't photographed TV images before, compare the meter's exposure recommendation with data in the table. Some light meters do not read TV or computer screen images accurately. If there is a significant discrepancy, set exposure according to the table. For more assurance of proper exposure, bracket the estimated exposure by plus or minus 1 or 2 stops using 1/2-stop increments. Note that for best color rendition with color films, you should use a color compensating filter, which entails an exposure increase from the settings listed in the table. See the table above for filter recommendations. For KODAK INSTAGRAPHIC Color Print Film see the instructions that come with the KODAK INSTAGRAPHIC Imager.

You can use the same exposures given in the table to photograph your home computer screen. If the screen displays images in full color, use the exposures in the table for color television and computer screens. If the screen is monochrome and displays images in black-and-white or tinted in one color, such as green, use the exposures for black-and-white television and computer screens.

It's a good idea to bracket the exposure until you're familiar with your equipment. A computer display image comprised of a white or a very light color background may require 1/2 to 1 stop less exposure than suggested in the table and a display image that shows a black or very dark color may require 1/2 to 1 1/2 stops more exposure than given in the table.

Bruce Nett

To capture the entire television or computer screen image uniformly, use shutter speeds no faster than 1/8 second with a focal-plane shutter or 1/30 second with a leaf shutter. The pictures above were made on EKTACHROME 400 Film (Daylight) with a focal-plane shutter 35 mm SLR. The one on the top was exposed for 1/8 second at f/11. The one on the bottom was exposed for 1/125 second at f/2.8, and has failed to record the image uniformly.

Suitable Shutter Speeds

TV and computer screen images are formed on the television or computer image tube (also referred to as cathode ray tube—CRT) line by line by a rapidly moving electron beam that scans the television picture or computer image. Therefore, you have to select a relatively slow shutter speed to give the beam time to form a complete, uniform image during the exposure. In the U.S., to obtain a uniform image, use a shutter speed no faster than 1/30 second with a leaf-shutter camera and no faster than 1/8 second with a camera that has a focal-plane shutter. In other countries that have standardized on a 625-line TV picture in preference to the U.S. 525-line picture, use a leaf-shutter speed no faster than 1/25 second

or a focal-plane shutter speed no faster than 1/8 second. Since 1/30 second is so close to 1/25 second, try the 1/30 setting with your leaf-shutter camera to see if you get a complete TV image. If not, you'll have to use 1/15 second or slower.

If you use a camera with a focal-plane shutter but want to record moderate on-screen action more sharply than a 1/8-second exposure permits, you can try 1/15- or 1/30-second exposures with corresponding adjustments in lens aperture. Some slight streaking will be evident in the pictures.

Variations in TV sets also make it advisable to bracket exposures until experience has verified good working data for your particular set and picture preferences. You may also wish to experiment with color filtration and/or the color adjustments of your TV set to obtain optimum color quality with color slide films. Because of the slow shutter speeds required to record a uniform image, time your exposures to coincide with peaks or lulls in on-screen action.

Copyright Considerations

Many television programs, video tapes, videodiscs, video games, and computer screen images are copyrighted. Taking pictures of images or making video or sound recordings of copyrighted materials also might be subject to copyright. As responsibility for complying with copyright laws must remain with the person taking the photograph or making the recording of a specific television program, image, or sound, Eastman Kodak Company can take no responsibility for copyright matters.

Existing-Light Photography in Public Places

There is a world of pictures waiting to be made outside the home, and many present themselves only to existing-light photographers. Indoors and outdoors, down the street or halfway around the world, subjects of interest abound. Some, like creatures of the night, cannot be found by day. And others, Cinderella-like, may be drab by day but radiant after dark. On the following pages are suggestions for photographing a variety of existing-light subjects and practical tips on how to do it.

Dusk, when there is still color in the sky, is a good time to photograph skylines and other illuminated night subjects. Make a reflected-light reading of the sky; then give about 1/2 or 1 stop less exposure than the meter indicates to keep the sky dark in the picture. This photograph was made on KODACOLOR VR 1000 Film.

Bruce Nett

81

Bruce Nett

For outdoor night photography, it's convenient to use a very high speed film so as to be prepared for various subject opportunities. Here the photographer chose EKTACHROME P800/1600 Professional Film (Daylight), EI 800, so he could shoot with a handheld camera set at a small lens opening for adequate depth of field. Sodium-vapor airport lighting.

OUTDOOR SCENES AT NIGHT

For the most part, outdoor scenes at night consist of highlight areas and dark areas, with few or no middle tones separating them. The highlights are nearly always the true subjects. Base your exposures primarily on highlight and middle-tone readings and don't allow large masses of dark surroundings to "trick" your exposure meter into recommending overexposure. Use high-speed film for handheld picture-taking or be prepared to use a tripod or an improvised camera support for longer exposures with slower films. And take along a small flashlight to shed light on exposure meter scales and camera settings and a small notebook to keep track of exposures used and other data. Early evening, when the lights are on and there is still some color in the sky, is a good time to shoot city skylines and large subjects, such as buildings and monuments, with a deep-blue sky or orange sunset background.

Street Scenes

Shopping thoroughfares and entertainment districts are rich in after-dark existing-light subjects. Since light sources are a mixed bag; you can make attractive overall shots on either daylight- or tungsten-balanced color slide films, depending on whether you prefer the warmer rendition of the former or the cooler look of the latter. It's a good idea to carry both types of film with you, though, because close-in pictures isolating specific areas may look decidedly better on one type of film than another. This is particularly true when people are prominent and you want to avoid excessively warm or cold skin tone. For photographing window displays, tungsten color slide films are usually compatible with display illumination. When in doubt or when you want color prints, use one of the KODACOLOR Films which produce generally excellent results in night photography. For black-and-white prints, TRI-X Pan Film is a superb film for outdoor night scenes.

If you have two camera bodies or two cameras, load one with daylight-balanced color slide film, for example, and the other with a tungsten-balanced slide film or perhaps a high-speed color negative or black-and-white film. That way you're ready for virtually any lighting condition within reason. Identify the film type in each camera body prominently. Many 35 mm SLRs are equipped with frames on the camera back that will accept the end flap from a film carton as a reminder of the film in use. If your camera doesn't have a film-reminder device of some sort, stick a good-sized strip of masking tape on the back cover or camera base, and write the film type on it with a bold marker so you can read it easily in dim light.

If you don't have two 35 mm camera bodies, you can change to a different film in the middle of the roll. You can do this with a 35 mm camera, before opening the camera back, by first noting the number of exposures on the camera frame counter, and then carefully rewinding the film, but not completely, so the leader sticks out of the film magazine for reloading. By rewinding slowly and carefully, you can tell when the film leader pulls loose from the take-up spool. Then you can load a different kind of film in the camera.

Caroline Grimes

You can use tungsten- or daylight-balanced color slide films to photograph street scenes at night. The former produce cooler rendition, the latter warmer-looking colors. This scene was photographed on tungsten-balanced EKTACHROME 160 Film (Tungsten) top and daylight-balanced EKTACHROME 400 Film (Daylight) bottom. Exposures were 1/30 second at f/4 and 1/60 second at f/4, respectively.

Caroline Grimes

Tungsten-balanced color slide films usually produce attractive color rendition under the tungsten light used to illuminate many display windows. Here the photographer used EKTACHROME 160 Film (Tungsten), 1/30 second at f/2.8.

Later when you reload the original, partially exposed film magazine, load it exactly like you did the first time. Then with the camera back closed and a lens cap or your hand tightly covering the lens, advance the film to the same number of frames that were on the camera film counter the first time plus two more, so that double exposures from reloading are not likely. During reloading be sure to advance the film adequately to duplicate the number of frames you advanced the film for loading the first time in addition to the number of frames that were exposed before taking additional pictures.

Plan nocturnal picture prowls to coincide with an area's peak of activity. If you show up too early, too late, or on an off night, the scene may be depopulated with few lights in evidence. But then, that could make an interesting picture, too, and an unexpected counter to the conventional view.

Don't let less-than-perfect weather stop you from seeking street pictures at night. Rain-slick surfaces and pools of water reflect lights attractively. Sometimes the reflections are even more interesting than the subjects they represent.

Michael Hendrix

The busiest shopping and entertainment areas will be deserted if you arrive too early, too late, or on an off evening. On the other hand, a picture showing a normally bustling street in a quiet mood can be effective, too. KODACOLOR VR 1000 Film, 1/30 second, f/2.8.

Wet streets after a rainstorm add interest to night scenes by reflecting lights and illuminated signs. Sometimes the reflections can make an intriquing and colorful picture.

Don Chamberlin

A tripod-mounted camera and long exposures of several seconds let you record patterns and trails formed by the lights of moving traffic after dark. You can use KODACOLOR Films for color prints, or daylight- or tungsten-balanced color slide films, depending on whether you prefer warmer or cooler color slide rendition.

Neil Montanus

Traffic Patterns

Headlights and taillights of moving autos can trace interesting patterns on film during long exposures. The effects you can record are limited only by the traffic arteries available, your viewpoint, and your imagination. A single car moving along an otherwise deserted avenue, a look down at a busy intersection or freeway cloverleaf, views of expressway traffic from an overpass—wherever there are cars and roadways you'll find subject matter for nighttime pictures.

For long, flowing streaks of light, use exposures long enough to allow the images of the light sources to move far enough on the film to produce the desired effect. An exposure of about 30 seconds usually works well with car traffic. Be alert to traffic light cycles so you don't record stationary vehicles stopped for a red light. Using exposure times that require a camera support means you can use films such as KODACHROME 64 Film (Daylight), ISO (ASA) 64, or even KODACHROME 40 Film 5070 (Type A), ISO (ASA) 40. You can use faster films, too, by selecting smaller lens apertures that allow longer exposure times. For warm results when you want color slides, select daylight-balanced slide film. For cooler rendition, choose a tungsten film. If you want color prints and you'd like the option of deciding on specific color rendition after the fact by doing your own printing in the darkroom, use KODACOLOR Film.

If a street scene or lighted monument is prominent in the background, choose an overall exposure level that will render it as you prefer while allowing a long enough exposure to register light trails of the desired length. For example, if you would normally expose KODACOLOR VR 400 Film at 1/15 second and f/2 to record the monument, you could achieve approximately the same exposure level for the monument at 4 seconds and f/11, allowing plus 1 stop for reciprocity characteristics, to capture longer trails of moving lights.

Exposure times required for good streak effects are too long for handheld photography. Use a tripod or improvised support to steady your camera. Bracket exposures profusely until you develop a sixth sense about suitable shutter speeds or exposure times for the situations you prefer to photograph. Unless there is important subject matter of known color in the scene, don't worry about correcting moderate color shifts resulting from reciprocity effects. Moderately long exposures of about 30 seconds will cause some reciprocity effects with many films, but they will be minimal and the results are usually acceptable for outdoor night subjects, which are less critical regarding precise color rendition. Lighting near most streets and highways isn't conducive to literal color rendition in any case. Do compensate for loss of film speed if the table on page 61 indicates that a discrepancy of 1 stop or more is likely.

Holiday Lighting

Religious and secular holidays are often marked by festive lighting displays that invite photography. Brightly colored lights and ornaments adorn trees, shop windows, main avenues, houses, and front yards. Choose film and exposure as you would for any other subject consisting primarily of light sources. You can embellish your photographs by shooting through any of the numerous star-effect filters available through photo dealers. These filters produce spikes of light that radiate from bright lights. They are most effective when a discrete light source appears against a dark background. Wide lens apertures produce thicker, softer-edged radial patterns and more diffusion. Stopping down slightly to moderate apertures thins the radial patterns and renders them and the image sharper. Don't stop down too far, though, or the star effect may be lost. If you use an SLR camera with a depth-of-field preview mechanism, judge the star pattern with the lens stopped down to shooting aperture, and open or close the diaphragm as necessary to control the effect.

Holiday lights create interesting reflections in wet weather, and they cast subtle colors on clean snow. In cold weather, keep your camera under your coat when you're not actually using it. Batteries and internal mechanisms may become sluggish if exposed to very cold temperatures for prolonged periods of time.

Gary Whelpley

Arthur Ketchum

To emphasize the water flow, photograph an illuminated fountain at a slow shutter speed or long exposure with a tripod-mounted camera. To obtain the blurred water effect, you can use an exposure time of 4 seconds.

Star-effect filters available through photo dealers can turn bright lights into dazzling star patterns. The effect is most pronounced when the light source appears against a dark or black background. This photograph, taken during Octoberfest, was made on KODACHROME 64 Film (Daylight).

Bruce Nett

Bright holiday lights are perfect subjects for existing-light photographs. With fast film, you can use shutter speeds fast enough for handheld photography. KODACOLOR VR 400 Film, 1/60 second f/4.

Floodlighted Structures

Buildings, monuments, statues, and fountains of special scenic, historic, or civic interest are often illuminated by floodlights. The dramatic lighting effects sometimes make the structure look better by night than by day. Normal exposure-meter techniques produce good exposure results provided you take care not to include light sources in the meter field when the structure itself is the subject of interest, and provided you make close-up readings of the subject to avoid the dark surround of the night sky. A film with an ISO (ASA) speed of 400 will usually allow exposures on the order of 1/15 second or 1/30 second at f/2, so you may be able to make handheld pictures when using fast normal or wide-angle lenses. Fountains that feature eye-catching water jets or cascades may look more dramatic if you photograph them with a tripod-mounted camera at a relatively slow shutter speed or time exposure to blur the water flow enough to convey the feeling of motion.

KODAK Pathe'

Historic buildings and monuments are often floodlighted after dark. Normal exposure meter techniques work well, but don't read the lights themselves, which cause underexposure, or the black night sky, which causes overexposure.

Robert Sullivan, SKPA

Bruce Nett

Outdoor Sports at Night

Well-lighted outdoor stadiums and playing fields offer excellent opportunities to make dramatic photographs of sports action ranging from neighborhood softball games to professional auto races. Light sources may be tungsten, daylight-quality Multi-Vapor lighting, or possibly mercury-vapor lamps.

In bright tungsten lighting, use EKTACHROME 160 Film (Tungsten) for most realistic rendition on color slides, push-processing it if necessary to gain the extra film speed you need to stop action. In Multi-Vapor lighting, use EKTACHROME 400 Film (Daylight) and EKTACHROME P800/1600 Professional Film (Daylight) for well-balanced color slides, and push process them if required. With mercury-vapor lamps, use a high-speed, daylight-balanced color slide film if you must have transparencies, although as indicated in the chapter on Kodak films, color rendition is problematical. KODACOLOR VR 400 and KODACOLOR VR 1000 Films are excellent choices with all three light sources. For black-and-white prints, you can choose TRI-X Pan Film. If you need a higher speed film to let you use higher shutter speeds to stop action in dim light, you can push-process the film so you can expose it at a higher film-speed number. Or you can use KODAK Recording Film 2475 or ROYAL-X Pan Film, depending on the size film your camera accepts.

Try to find a shooting position close enough to the action so you won't need long focal-length telephoto lenses, which magnify camera movement along with the image. And if you cannot use shutter speeds fast enough to stop subject motion adequately, make exposures coincide with peak action or picturesque lulls. Alternatively, you could pan with the action as described on page 24.

If you cannot use a shutter speed fast enough to freeze the action or if you want some movement in the picture to heighten the impression of speed, use a slower shutter speed and pan the camera with the moving subject. This picture was made by panning with the subject at 1/30 second and f/4 on 400 speed KODACOLOR Film.

Neil Montanus

Outdoor playing fields, stadiums, and racetracks are usually lighted well enough to permit making action-stopping photographs with high-speed films. Here the photographer caught the action at 1/500 second and f/2.8 on KODACOLOR VR 1000 Film.

Lighted action rides at amusement parks and carnivals trace interesting patterns during long exposures. Mount the camera on a tripod. This picture was exposed for 4 seconds on KODACHROME 64 Film (Daylight).

Fairs and Amusement Parks

Outdoors at night it's the colorful lighting that sets the mood at fairs and amusement parks, and makes good pictures. You can easily take handheld exposures of interesting arrays of lights with fast film. For pictures that go a bit beyond the ordinary, try photographing lighted action rides and Ferris wheels with a tripod-mounted camera at exposure times slow enough to record swirls and patterns formed by the moving lights. With color slide films, select the balance to suit your taste: daylight films for warmer results, tungsten films for cooler colors. KODACOLOR Films give excellent photos of these subjects. If you do your own darkroom work or have your prints made by a custom processing laboratory, KODACOLOR Films will let you choose the balance you like. In crowded areas or on action rides, sling your camera so that it nestles between your arm and side for protection from bumps.

Fireworks and Lightning

Taking pictures of fireworks displays or lightning is a form of flash photography in reverse. Instead of photographing what the flash illuminates, you're photographing the flash itself.

You can photograph aerial fireworks best with a tripod-mounted camera. Aim your camera at the area where most bursts are occurring, set focus on infinity, and set the lens opening as suggested in the table on page 42. Set the shutter to B, open it when a burst blossoms, and keep it open until you have collected several successive bursts on the same frame of film. If you don't have a tripod, camera settings of 1/30 second and *f*/2.8 for ISO (ASA) 200 films, such as EKTACHROME 200 Film (Daylight), permit making handheld shots of individual bursts. With slower or faster films, increase or reduce the exposure appropriately. If you're using an autofocus camera, set the focus manually on infinity, if possible. See your camera manual. If you can't set the focus manually, take a test shot of the fireworks and then check the focus indicator to determine whether your camera is focusing properly on infinity. Infinity is indicated by a figure eight on its side ∞ or by a distant scene symbol, such as mountains.

If your camera has a multiple-exposure control that lets you make more than one exposure on a single film frame, you can collect several bursts in one picture by making multiple exposures. With this multiple-exposure technique, be sure to aim your camera at the sky so it doesn't include any objects on the ground that would cause confusing multiple ground images. You can also use your hat to cover the lens between bursts while you're waiting for the next one to occur without having to close the camera shutter.

Fireworks displays over water create colorful reflections on the surface. Enhance your pictures by photographing both the displays and their reflections for more interesting effects. Include a skyline, foreground object, or possibly an illuminated monument in the frame to lend an added sense of dimension. Use a medium telephoto lens to fill the frame dramatically when you can use a tripod and you have a good idea where the bursts will occur. If you want to use a

Arthur Ketchum

You can put more visual interest in pictures of fireworks displays by collecting several bursts on each frame of film. You can do this with a tripod-mounted camera with the shutter open at the B setting. Or you can take several successive multiple exposures of individual bursts with a handheld camera. See text for details. You can take a picture like this on KODACOLOR VR 400 Film with your camera mounted on a tripod, shutter set on B, and lens aperture at f/16.

telephoto lens without a tripod, brace the camera as best you can for added steadiness or camera movement may mar the intricate tracery of the bursts.

You can record fairly static ground displays of fireworks well with shutter speeds fast enough for handholding your camera. Select exposure settings from the table on page 42. Daylight color films render fireworks very attractively for most tastes.

Photographing lightning bolts is like photographing fireworks except there is a greater element of chance, as you don't know exactly where the flash will be or when it will come. Mount your camera on a tripod and use a normal or wide-angle lens to include a good expanse of likely target area. Set the lens to an appropriate aperture as suggested in the table on page 42 and hold the shutter open at the B setting long enough to record several flashes. For safety's sake, take lightning photographs from indoors through a window or doorway or from some other substantial shelter. Don't under any circumstances station yourself outdoors in the open with a tripod when lightning conditions exist because you or the tripod could become a lightning rod. And don't take cover under a tree, either. Trees attract lightning strikes, too. A safer place to be is in a car with a metal top but don't touch any metal parts of the car.

When you have to keep the shutter open for awhile until you collect several flashes, try to exclude lighted areas from the frame. If lights of passing vehicles impinge on the picture area, either plan your picture to use the streaks as part of the design, or cover the lens with a black card or even a hat to keep the intrusions from recording on film. Uncover the lens again when the intruder has left the field. You can also use this lens covering technique in between fireworks bursts when you want to record several bursts on the same frame of film.

Several lightning flashes look more dramatic on film than one. Mount your camera on a tripod with the shutter open at B, and aim it in the direction of the storm. Close the shutter after several strong bolts have flashed in the picture field. Photograph from indoors or a substantial shelter. Never remain in the open when lightning is in the area. For color prints, you could use KODACOLOR VR 400 Film, shutter open on B, and aperture set to f/11.

EXISTING-LIGHT PICTURES INDOORS IN PUBLIC PLACES

The materials and methods you're accustomed to using when making existing-light pictures indoors at home are equally applicable to picture-taking indoors in public places. One important difference, though, is that making pictures in public places requires a bit more forethought. Try to anticipate shooting conditions so you will arrive prepared. You won't be able to step into the next room for an extra roll of film or one of a different type, and you cannot simply retrieve your tripod from the hall closet when you're across town or half a country away from home. Another difference is that you will rarely have the option of altering the environment to improve the photographic conditions. You aren't free to change stage lighting, rearrange furnishings in a restaurant, or move a display in a museum or gallery to a spot with better lighting. These constraints notwithstanding, you can make pleasing photographs of events, activities, objects, and settings you encounter in many public places. Consider the following possibilities.

Museums and Art Galleries

Art objects, artifacts, and dramatic dioramas are inviting subjects in art galleries and museums. In the more modern facilities, display lighting is often artfully arranged to bring out the best in the illuminated objects, making them easy to photograph well. If you have a macro lens or other close-focusing optic, be sure to take it with you to help isolate small objects and eliminate surrounding clutter. A wide-angle lens can be helpful for photographing large three-dimensional displays and dioramas. It lets you take in the area you want to cover without having to back up so far that other visitors keep getting between you and the subject. Sometimes there's not enough space to move back far enough to include what you want in the photo when you're using a normal focal length lens.

If you're shooting color slides, take both daylight- and tungsten-balanced films with you. It isn't uncommon to encounter, in a single museum, galleries illuminated by skylight, others illuminated by fluorescent tubes, and still others lighted by tungsten sources. In fact, mixed lighting may be found quite often, too. Don't be surprised if the area lighting is provided by skylights or fluorescent fixtures while individual displays are bathed by small tungsten spot- and floodlights. Choose the film according to the lighting that affects the specific subject you're photographing. Two cameras loaded with films of different balance make it easier to win the lighting game. Or load a single camera with EKTACHROME 160 Film (Tungsten) and take along a No. 85B conversion filter for use with daylight or fluorescent lights. If you push the film 1 stop, you can rate it at ISO (ASA) 320 with no filter and ISO (ASA) 200 with the filter, which should be fast enough for many museum and gallery light levels. When you would like color prints, KODACOLOR VR 400 Film has ample speed to cope with displays that are adequately lighted for good viewing. For brightly lighted areas you can use this same film or KODACOLOR VR 200 Film.

Don't count on using a tripod or flash unit to supplement existing light. Most museums and galleries prohibit the use of a tripod and some prohibit the use of flash. Check with the staff ahead of time

Museums and art galleries offer a wealth of subjects to existing-light photographers. As a rule, objects are lighted better for photography than are paintings and drawings. EKTACHROME 160 Film (Tungsten) with ESP-1 Processing, ISO (ASA) 320.

A close-focusing or macro lens is handy for isolating small objects and displays from distracting surroundings. This close view was made on KODACOLOR VR 1000 Film.

Keep your eye on other visitors, too. Their reactions to exhibits can provide engaging human-interest pictures. The photographer caught this moment on KODACOLOR VR 1000 Film, 1/30 second at f/2.

to be sure. If you're lucky, you may be able to obtain special permission. Although, with the excellent high-speed films and high-speed lenses that are available today, you can usually take existing-light pictures using a handheld camera without flash. Keep this advantage of existing-light photography in mind; it's least disturbing to the picture-taking environment. Some museums require paying a nominal extra fee if you wish to take pictures and some do not allow photography at all. Again, checking ahead of time will avoid disappointment.

In the majority of museums that do permit photography, look beyond the exhibits for subjects. Other visitors and their reactions to exhibits can provide engaging human interest. As far as photographing paintings is concerned, it is very difficult to do well in the context of informal existing-light photography. You will usually do better by buying an inexpensive copy or postcard of the painting at the museum gift shop and using your film to record objects and people.

Circuses and Ice Shows

Exuberant performers and blazing colors make ice shows and circuses photogenic acts that are hard to top. Try to get seats with a good view of the part of the arena where acts in which you are most interested are scheduled to perform. If there is a printed program, browse through it ahead of time to help pace your shooting. You don't want to be changing film at the height of the action. If your seats are farther from ring- or rinkside than you'd like, use a fast telephoto or zoom lens of moderate focal length to tighten composition. And use the highest shutter speeds you can to stop whirling figure skaters or swooping aerialists.

Light levels are generally high enough to permit using shutter speeds from 1/60 second to 1/250 second at f/2.8 with ISO (ASA) 400 films. The lower end of the speed range is appropriate to tungsten-lighted areas, the higher end for main events spotlighted by carbon arcs. Daylight-type color slide films produce realistic color rendition under carbon-arc spotlighting while tungsten films yield more accurate color balance under tungsten illumination. If it isn't convenient or practical for you to use both types, use a daylight-balanced film for everything.

Neil Montanus

High-speed film let the photographer use a fast shutter speed to stop the tiger performing at the circus. KODACOLOR VR 1000 Film, ISO 1000, was exposed for 1/250 second at f/3.5. A moderate telephoto lens helped bridge the distance from seat to action. Alberto Zoppe' produced Circus Europa.

Martin Czamanske

In light bright enough for exposures of about 1/100 second at f/2.8 with ISO 200 film, you can make existing-light pictures with KODAK Disc Cameras. If you don't want the built-in flash to affect the picture, block the flash window with a swatch of tape. This picture was made with a KODAK Disc Camera and KODAK Disc Film. The flash was not blocked, but contributed very little light for the subjects because they are so far away. The picture was made mainly by the existing light. M&M Circus International.

89

KODACOLOR VR 400 and KODACOLOR VR 1000 Films produce excellent results all around. When special multi-colored lighting effects are part of an act, you'll get arresting pictures regardless of the type of color film in your camera.

The bright lighting at circuses and ice shows will also let you take existing-light pictures with disc cameras that have fast lenses, such as KODAK Disc Cameras, and KODACOLOR VR Disc Film. For many pictures of the acts at the circus or ice show, you'll be far enough from your subjects so the built-in flash won't actually affect the exposure, which will be completely by existing light. At the flash exposure of 1/100 second at f/2.8, automatically determined by a KODAK Disc Camera, KODACOLOR VR Disc Film, ISO 200, has enough speed to yield quality prints of brightly lighted acts beyond the flash distance range.

At ice shows, the surface of the ice is highly reflective and can trick reflected-light exposure meters into indicating camera settings that would underexpose less-bright scene elements such as performers. See text for details. This correctly exposed photograph was made on KODACOLOR VR 400 Film, 1/125 second at f/2.8 at Ice Capades, Inc.

Since the camera automatically controls the flash, it will fire unless the existing lighting is very bright. When the subject is closer to the camera and within the flash distance range of 4 to 18 feet, depending on the camera, the photo will look like a flash picture with some detail in the background provided by the existing lighting. When the subject is beyond

the maximum flash distance range beginning at about 18 feet, the picture will look more like an existing-light picture when the existing lighting is bright enough for proper exposure.

If you want to take pictures solely by the existing light with a KODAK Disc Camera, when the subject is within the flash distance range and is adequately lighted by the existing lighting, you can block the flash window with a strip of black masking tape. If in doubt, take two pictures—one with the flash and another one with the flash window blocked to determine the technique you like best. Keep in mind that the existing light has to be bright enough to use the no flash technique with disc cameras.

You can take existing-light photographs successfully with KODAK Disc Cameras and KODACOLOR VR Disc Film, ISO 200, in light levels that permit an exposure setting of approximately 1/100 second at f/2.8, or less exposure. Refer to the exposure tables on pages 42 and 43.

At ice shows, the high reflectivity of the ice does two things. It lightens shadows usefully by bouncing light into them. And somewhat less usefully, it can induce reflected-light exposure meters to recommend camera settings that will underexpose scene elements that are less reflective than the ice. If there are lots of performers in the exposure meter's field of view, enough ice will be covered to negate the problem. However, if you make a reading when there are few performers and a vast expanse of bare ice in view, set the camera for about 1/2 to 1 stop more exposure than the meter suggests. Experience will help you to decide how much correction to make.

A good exposure technique to keep in mind for performers that are more brightly lighted than the surroundings, such as when spotlights are being used, is to put a telephoto lens on your camera with through-the-lens exposure metering. This lets you make close-up readings when you can't get close enough to the subjects to do it with a normal-focal length lens. Then replace the telephoto with the normal lens to shoot the picture. An overall meter reading for these conditions would overexpose the more brightly lighted subjects. Another alternative is to use the exposure in the table on page 43.

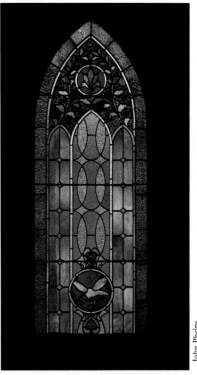

The brilliant colors and intricate designs of stained-glass windows show up best when they are illuminated by daylight shining through them. Use daylight-balanced color film for realistic color rendition. This photograph was made on KODACHROME 64 Film (Daylight) exposed for 1/30 second at f/4.

Houses of Worship

Some of life's more memorable moments may occur in houses of worship, and unobtrusive existing-light photography lets you preserve them without diminishing the dignity of the proceedings. A good location to shoot from is the first row of the balcony, if there is one. You'll have a good overall view and you can rest the camera on a railing for additional support. Use a normal or wide-angle lens for general views, and a fast telephoto or zoom lens to close in on key events near the altar.

Lighting may be daylight, tungsten, or both. Choose your film accordingly. With mixed light sources, use a color slide film that is balanced for the dominant source. If you need prints, a KODACOLOR Film will cope well with any lighting you're likely to encounter.

When traveling, you may wish to photograph interiors of churches and other houses of worship noted for their architectural beauty or historic significance. A high-speed wide-angle lens will prove invaluable for framing soaring arches, and a medium focal-length telephoto will let you isolate details of interest. Stained-glass windows are especially pictureworthy. They look best when

90

photographed from inside the structure, transilluminated by daylight. Make a reflected-light reading of the window only, excluding from the meter field darker surroundings that could result in erroneous exposure data. If you cannot make a close enough reading or your exposure meter is not working properly, try an exposure 3 stops greater than what you would use for prevailing outdoor lighting conditions. For example, with the sun shining on the window and an ISO (ASA) 400 film in your camera, instead of exposing for 1/500 second at $f/16$ as you would outdoors in bright sunlight, expose the stained-glass window from inside for 1/125 second at $f/11$.

Whenever you contemplate making photographs in a house of worship, it is a good idea to make sure first that doing so will not be considered a breach of good taste or perhaps an offense against a deeply held religious belief. If a ceremony is in progress, be as inconspicuous as possible so as not to distract from the proceedings. On a more secular note, if you attend a wedding where a professional photographer has been engaged, don't let your picture-taking efforts interfere with his or hers. Rest assured that there will be more than enough picture opportunities for everyone.

Existing-Light Photography En Route

When you're traveling, the experiences you encounter in your mode of transportation itself may provide some fond memories in addition to those at your destination. Take pictures of friends, family, and other traveling companions en route in motor vehicles, trains, planes, and boats. No means of transportation is too far out. Even astronauts photograph each other in flight.

Daylight transmitted through windows and portholes is the best light source, and is usually bright enough to allow using reasonably high shutter speeds in conjunction with fast films. Use daylight-type color films unless the vehicle has deeply tinted windows. In that event, use black-and-white film or take pictures with flash. Select the fastest shutter speed conditions permit, because vehicular motion causes random, unpredictable camera movement. Hold your camera as steadily as you can and take pictures during smooth intervals rather

Houses of worship are the settings for many of life's memorable events, which are natural subjects for unobtrusive existing-light photography. This photograph of a wedding was made on KODACOLOR VR 1000 Film, 1/125 second at f/4.

Don Maggio

Bruce Nett

than when traversing cobblestone paving or in rough air when the seat-belt sign is on. To prevent vibration from degrading image quality, don't brace your hands, arms, or your camera against any part of the vehicle. Normal exposure metering techniques work well except when a window is behind the person you're photographing. In this situation, make a close-up reading of the subject.

Keep your camera at hand en route in your means of transportation to record additional aspects of a trip. Daylight coming through the windows of an airliner was bright enough for an exposure of 1/125 second at f/4 on KODACOLOR VR 400 Film. Expose at the highest practical shutter speed considering depth-of-field requirements to counter vehicular motion and vibration.

School Events

Whether you're a parent or a student, school events such as parties, dances, award ceremonies, concerts, plays, and athletic competitions are rich in picture subjects. These events are memorable occasions, which make the pictures you take more valuable especially when family members are participants. Light sources may include window light during the day, or tungsten, fluorescent, or high-intensity discharge lamps in areas that are normally illuminated by artificial lights. If you aren't familiar with the area where you expect to be making pictures, a telephone call to school authorities ahead of time will usually elicit information about the type of lighting. Choose your film according to criteria for achieving correct color balance presented in the chapter on Kodak films. If you're taking pictures for a school newspaper or yearbook, black-and-white is the usual requirement so you'll want to use a high-quality black-and-white film well suited for existing-light photos. TRI-X Pan Film is an excellent choice.

Bruce Nett

Martin Czamanske

Daylight and fluorescent, KODACOLOR *VR 1000 Film.*

Martin Czamanske

Daylight and tungsten, KODACOLOR *VR 400 Film.*

Be ready for varied lighting when you photograph school activities. Daylight, tungsten illumination, and fluorescent tubes can all be found, separately or together. If you haven't visited the premises previously, check ahead of time to determine the type of lighting where you'll be photographing.

Indoor Sports

Sports action, professional or amateur, offers abundant opportunities to make exciting photographs. Find out in advance the type of lighting in use and choose color films to match. You should favor high-speed films, such as KODACOLOR VR 1000, KODACOLOR VR 400, EKTACHROME P800/1600 Professional (Daylight), EKTACHROME 400 (Daylight), EKTACHROME 160 (Tungsten) with push processing, and TRI-X Pan, ROYAL-X Pan, and 2475 Recording Film. In tungsten lighting, push-processing EKTACHROME 160 Film (Tungsten) 1 stop is desirable for higher speed and better action-stopping capability.

If your seat or shooting location is far from the playing area, a medium telephoto lens can bring you closer optically.

Indoor sports are most easily handled with high-speed film and fast lenses. KODACOLOR *VR 1000 Film, ISO 1000, combines very high sensitivity with excellent color response under a wide range of light sources. It was used to make this picture under Multi-Vapor lighting, at 1/250 second at f/2.8.*

You can blur motion deliberately to emphasize speed. Simply select a shutter speed or exposure time too slow to stop the action. See the table on page 24. This photograph was made on KODACHROME *25 Film (Daylight), 4 seconds, f/4, while panning the camera with the subjects.*

Jeff Nicholas, KINSA

Lenses with large maximum apertures are best. Use high shutter speeds to stop subject and camera movement. The most dependable exposure meter readings require access to the playing area before the event to make either close-up reflected-light measurements or incident-light readings. If that isn't possible, take care that reflected-light readings at a distance don't include excessive amounts of darker areas, such as sidelines and bleachers, or lighter areas, such as ice. If the playing surface is unusually light in tone and affects the meter reading, increase exposure about 1/2 or 1 stop more than the meter indicates. Set exposure before the action starts so you won't have to fiddle with camera controls during key moments when you should be devoting total attention to your subjects. If the playing area is lighted unevenly, note basic exposure settings to use in important lighter and darker zones. Don't worry about lighting variations that don't exceed 1 stop.

In light levels that preclude using high shutter speeds, shoot during momentary pauses or peaks in the action, such as the top of a basketball player's jump. Also remember that you can stop movement directly toward or away from you with slower shutter speeds than you can with movement crossing the lens field of view. You can capture rapid lateral motion dramatically by panning with it, as described on page 24. And don't overlook the possibility of making dramatically different motion shots in which the moving subject's speed is emphasized by deliberate blurring. To do this, use a shutter speed too slow to stop the moving subject, or for even more blur, pan the camera *opposite* the subject's direction of motion during the exposure. Experiment to find the shutter speeds and the panning motion that produce effects you like.

When attending sports events, it's easy to become totally involved with the action on the field. Nonetheless, keep an eye out for interesting picture possibilities in the stands, too. The antics of fans, their expressions when a favorite team or player scores or muffs a shot, the activities of refreshment and souvenir vendors, and the actions of the fans when the game ends all contribute to the overall spirit of the event. Look for these "bonus" subjects, because they sometimes prove more interesting than the players themselves.

Bruce Nett

Semi-close-up views of performers are especially rewarding. A medium telephoto lens helps bring you closer to the spectacle, as was the case here. KODACOLOR VR 1000 Film exposed for 1/125 second at f/4. A star-effect filter was used to produce the rays on the stage lights.

Stage Performances

You can make memorable photographs at plays and musical performances whether the stars are international celebrities or your neighbors from down the block. The front row of the balcony offers the best vantage point; you don't have to contend with heads blocking your view. In a large theater, bring along a medium telephoto lens to close the distance. From a strictly photographic standpoint, a dress rehearsal is preferable to an actual performance because you can move about discreetly to frame your shots to best advantage and you don't have to worry about interfering with other members of the audience. Stage lighting is compatible with tungsten color slide films. EKTACHROME 160 Film (Tungsten) is a good choice. Its ISO (ASA) 160 speed permits camera settings of approximately 1/60 second at f/4 for professionally lighted stage presentations. If you need more speed to stop dancers or rapid on-stage action, you can push-process the film for 1 or 2 stops higher speed as discussed on page 62. KODACOLOR VR 1000 Film and KODACOLOR VR 400 Film are logical choices for color prints. For black-and-white pictures, use TRI-X Pan Film.

Determining exposure for stage spectacles is best done ahead of time during a rehearsal with full lighting. Incident-light readings or close-up readings with a reflected-light exposure meter on stage are ideal. Reflected-light readings from the orchestra or balcony with a spot meter can be very accurate, too, provided you pin the spot on significant subject tones. Since light levels and effects may change frequently in the course of a performance, note in the program the exposure settings required for each scene or act. Stage lighting is often deliberately uneven to direct attention to specific areas of the stage. Set exposure to favor the important areas where the action takes place. Don't worry about minor fluctuations in light level of 1 stop or less. If you cannot make exposure readings in advance, rely on the suggested exposure data in the table on page 43 or on meter readings made during the show. Do not rely on reflected-light meter readings made from too far away from the stage which include the dark surroundings of the audience and the theater.

Since you will generally be photographing at a moderate distance from the stage, depth of field is likely to be adequate even at fairly wide lens apertures, so don't hesitate to use shutter speeds fast enough to stop action. In subdued lighting, wait for peaks or lulls in stage activity, as you would when photographing a sports event.

When shooting during an actual performance, don't let your photographic activities interfere with other audience members' enjoyment of the show. At recitals and concerts, don't trip the shutter during very soft passages or pauses. The click can be surprisingly disconcerting in a hushed hall. If you have a motor drive or autowinder, leave it at home because of the distracting noise these accessories generate.

A bonus of taking existing-light pictures is that you'll be less disruptive to the performance. This also means you won't be using flash. Taking flash pictures in a theater is very distracting to both the audience and the performers. Do not use flash unless express permission is given by the theater management. Better yet, leave your flash unit at home.

93

Do bring your pen-type flashlight for checking camera settings and reading notes you've jotted in the program. At professional theaters and concert halls all photography may be prohibited during performances. When that is the case, it is usually stated in the program. If you're not sure, ask theater personnel before curtain time and explain that you won't be using flash. Or make arrangements to take pictures during a dress rehearsal when you'll have much more freedom to move around.

Stage lighting is often uneven by design, to highlight performers and heighten drama. In general views, such as this one made on EKTACHROME 160 Film (Tungsten), 1/60 second, f/2.8, expose for the medium-tone and bright areas. When focusing in on details with a telephoto or zoom lens, adjust exposure to suit the specific area. Nutcracker Suite, courtesy New York City Ballet.

© Steven Caras, 1984

Neil Montanus

Lighting for floor shows can vary in color from moment to moment. When colored lighting effects or other light sources are part of the spectacle, don't worry about precise color balance because the pictures will likely be attractive and realistic. This shot was taken on KODACOLOR VR 1000 Film.

Night Clubs and Restaurants

A festive night out in your home town or while traveling offers existing-light picture possibilities in restaurants, cafés, or nightclubs. Lighting is normally tungsten and on the warm side to flatter patrons' complexions and look romantic. In addition, the lighting is often dim to create an intimate atmosphere, so take a fast tungsten-balanced color slide film such as EKTACHROME 160 Film (Tungsten). If you prefer to have color prints, KODACOLOR VR 1000 Film or KODACOLOR VR 400 Film, should be at the top of your list. Any of the Kodak black-and-white films with an ISO (ASA) speed of 400 or faster would be appropriate for black-and-white prints. Since light levels are often low to enhance mood, you should plan on push-processing EKTACHROME 160 Film (Tungsten) 1 or 2 stops.

Shooting distances are likely to be short to moderate, so stick to normal or wide-angle lenses with large maximum apertures unless you suspect you will be seated far from an interesting floor show. In that case, a medium telephoto will be helpful. If you have to use shutter speeds lower than 1/60 second, brace your camera on anything that's steadier than you are. Don't be overly concerned about color balance. A spectacular picture of the maître d' flaming crêpes suzette or of fancifully costumed dancers whirling under multi-colored spotlights will be accepted as is, with no quibbling about whether or not the color balance is less than optimum.

If the lighting is uneven, as is often the case, use exposures that favor middletone and highlight areas. Be careful not to "trick" your meter by aiming it at candles on the table or bright lights while making exposure readings. When in doubt, bracket. And don't be discouraged by rapid and essentially unpredictable changes in lighting during floor shows. Compensate as best you can and keep on shooting. Your goal, after all, is not to create a clinically precise record, but rather a meaningful memento of the moment. Take a penlight flashlight along to help you see your camera settings in the dim light.

Caroline Grimes

Expositions of all kinds are good stalking grounds for existing-light pictures. Lighting varies widely, and individual exhibits may be lighted differently from surrounding areas. If you shoot color slides, take tungsten- and daylight-balanced films to cover all possibilities. The photograph of a custom car show was made on EKTACHROME 160 Film (Tungsten) with ESP-1 Processing, ISO (ASA) 320.

Hobby and Trade Shows

Hobby and craft exhibitions, flower shows, business and trade shows, consumer-oriented automobile and boat shows, and expositions of all kinds are interesting places to take existing-light pictures. Lighting may be tungsten, fluorescent, or even Multi-Vapor or mercury vapor overall, and individual exhibit areas may have lighting that differs from the general area illumination. If you cannot find out in advance what the predominant light source is, hedge your bets by taking daylight- and tungsten-balanced color slide films, or a high-speed KODACOLOR or black-and-white film. Light levels are usually high enough to

permit photography with a handheld camera. No special metering techniques are normally required.

A lens that permits close focusing, or a simple supplementary lens attachment that extends the close-focusing ability of a fast normal or medium telephoto lens, will let you move in and make eye-catching close-ups of interesting details. Focus carefully and hold the camera steady when shooting close-ups. If possible, brace the camera on a firm support.

Besides photographing the displays, keep an eye on the interaction between exhibitors and visitors to add a human dimension. Also be on the lookout for good shots of people reacting to the

displays. You could make a charming picture story, for example, recording the expressions of children at a toy show or exhibitors grooming their pets at a dog show. Just be ready with your camera and an ample supply of film. The rest is a matter of careful observation and patience.

When you attend a meeting or a lecture, you can use existing-light techniques as a visual form of note taking. You can photograph displays, demonstrations, blackboards, and slides on a screen. Choose color or black-and-white film for your needs. For color slides of projected images, generally tungsten film is the best choice.

Recommended reading

The world of photography is so vast and varied that even the most experienced photographer finds surprises and challenges at every turn. It seems that everything you learn and every skill you acquire leads to still more things to learn and new skills to master. Each new answer brings with it a new question.

This book has presented a practical approach to existing-light photography, introducing you to working methods and materials with which you may not have been familiar previously. Because of the sheer impossibility of exploring in-depth all of the points touched on without straying too far from the main subject, some aspects of the discussion may have piqued your curiosity at least as much as they satisfied it.

The following Kodak publications are recommended to help you further along your voyage of photographic discovery. These and other helpful Kodak books on a variety of photographic subjects are available through your photo dealer. For a list of current titles and prices send for a free copy of *Photography Books from Kodak*, L-7. Address your request to:

Department 412-L
Eastman Kodak Company
Rochester, New York 14650

The Joy of Photographing People, AC-72H (hardcover), AC-72S (soft-cover)

The Joy of Photography, AC-75H (hardcover), AC-75S (soft-cover)

More Joy of Photography, AC-70H (hardcover), AC-70S (soft-cover)

KODAK Guide to 35 mm Photography, AC-95S

KODAK Pocket Photoguide, AR-21

KODAK Pocket Guide to 35 mm Photography, AR-22

KODAK Films—Color and Black-and-White, AF-1

KODAK Color Films for Professional Use, E-77

KODAK Professional Black-and-White Films, F-5

Picture credits
outside back cover

Bride—Don Maggio
Museum Display—Caroline Grimes
Sphinx—Norm Kerr

Index